ONE

Standing at the back of the audie
Chicken was in the pulsing, nervous ninterland of waiting to go on. They both watched as the compere did his best to whip up some enthusiasm in the cold and surly crowd who hadn't yet had quite enough beer. Beside him, Morgan, the headline act was getting very twitchy.
'That bald guy. Down the front. That bald git,' he was saying in a growl. Chicken hadn't noticed the guy but Morgan was alive to anything and everything that could give him a problem. As the veteran of thousands of shows, he knew full-well how little it took for the whole thing to end up in the toilet. The same act that went down so well the night before, in some other club in some other town, could always see you die the following night. You could never tell and sometimes it all started with an aggressively bald git and a few of his friends.
'Why is he sitting down the front if he doesn't want to laugh? Bald git.'
Chicken took a sideways look at Morgan's own shiny skull and murmured,
'Yeah you've got to watch the bald ones.'

The compere did ok, in a where-are-you-from, what-do-you-do-for-a-job, look-at-your-geeky-glasses kind of way. And then Chicken heard his cue,
'Are you ready for some comedy? Shall we bring a comedian out?'

Chicken's mouth suddenly felt very dry and he gulped from the glass of water that he was holding. No alcohol until he was finished, he'd made that mistake before. There was an urgent need to visit the toilet but he knew it to be a phantom urge and ignored it as he'd already experienced his ritualistic violent evacuation in the club's grotty cubicle. He began to walk through the tables towards the stage as some of the punters clapped and all craned their necks to see if they recognised the face. They didn't.

He knew after thirty seconds that it was going to be a hard work night but he didn't panic he ploughed on. Never let them know you're in pain he told himself while, what the hell am I doing up here? flashed through his mind. He had about half the crowd with him, the more discerning half he felt. He worked through his act for about twenty minutes which was his slot. He threw away a line and it got a good laugh so he pushed through to his big ending. He got a kind of grudgingly reasonable final response and he shuffled off relieved to be finished.

'Ok, let's hear it again for Chicken,' shouted the compere bounding back onto the stage.

At the back again, unnoticed, he watched as Morgan was introduced and ambled onstage where he immediately lost all trace of his apprehension as he took over the space. They loved him from his first grimace. For him, the whole crowd was a friend – well almost all. Attack is the best offence so he took the bald man on head to head, bald to bald and won. His set soared for a while, dipped slightly in the middle and then galloped in like a favourite. 40 minutes of variable laughter. Knob gags for drunks. Show business.

I wonder what will happen when the world runs dry of jokes? thought Chicken. How will we survive?

Chicken drove back with Morgan next to him to share the petrol cost. In the eerie post gig silence of the car each was alone and dissected his own performance. Unlike Chicken, as headliner Morgan had made just enough money to make it worthwhile. Eventually Chicken said, 'Comedy clubs are shit aren't they? I mean who are those people? Why aren't they at home watching Coronation Street?' Morgan didn't look at him.

'Your set was ok,' he answered. 'You maybe need to lose the bit about gangsters, not sure they knew where that was going. Not sure I did.'
'That's my favourite bit though. Not crude enough for that type of crowd maybe?'
'Yeah, or not funny enough.' They both laughed. Morgan was a pro. Over the years Morgan had developed what was described as a bullet proof set. No joke that he hadn't seen work a hundred times before. He looked sideways at the driver and decided to impart some comforting wisdom.
'When I first started I did a gong show in south London, and I went on last, so although they were a crap, pissed-up audience I just said, look, if you gong me off now your night is over so you might as well let me go on. And they liked that so they let me live and I went down really well. It was great, I felt like a king. So, Malcolm the club owner gave me another spot the next week. I went back and they booed me off after 30 seconds. Died on my arse. Went home and cried.'
There was a knowing pause.
'I didn't die tonight,' said Chicken. 'I did NOT die.'
'No. That's right.'

The house was dark when Chicken got in, his wife Laura asleep. She had zero interest in his comedy career, which suited him fine as he didn't want to talk about it anyway. Ironically, while audiences sank into trouser pissing inebriation, for a lot of performers gig nights were non-alcoholic because of the need to drive home. Now with a glass of vodka in hand he sat on the kitchen sofa, his brain too busy to sleep and went over every second of his act, sometimes wincing, occasionally smiling and nodding.

He already knew what would be dropped and what would be improved for the next gig. In truth there weren't many next gigs booked and he was aware that come the morning he'd have to hit the emails and phone calls hard. The prospect of the humiliating dance of kissing the arses of club promoters left him cold. As far as Chicken was concerned most promoters were failed comedians who only went into comedy club management to have comedians suck up to them. They liked to hear begging, the more pathetic the better.

When Chicken had dropped him off Morgan had mumbled something about getting in touch with 'something big' that was coming up. It had barely registered with him, comedians were the most unreliable people that Chicken knew, full of promises and lies. They all kept their contacts close to their chests, a bunch of jealous, selfish, self absorbed, thin-skinned wasters. That's what he loved about them their predictability. However, he made a mental note to chase Morgan up in a day or two. It may have been bullshit, but he could really do with something big right now.

Chicken looked up from his thoughts to see Laura standing in the doorway, her pink dressing gown wrapped tight, her hair in disarray.
'How'd it go?' It was an unusual question from her.
'Good, good. Well, pretty good.'
'Cool. You get paid?'
'Yeah. But not much.'
He looked at the drink in his hand. 'You want a drink?'
She shook her head. 'No, I've got work in a few hours.'
'Right.'
She turned to go so he threw her the golden nugget.
'Morgan, the headliner from tonight, reckons he might have something for me. Something big.'
She nodded again.
'Big,' he emphasised.
'Good. Let's hope it pays.'

For distraction he switched on the TV and heard a huge crackle of studio audience laughter. The show that blinded him in the gloom of the kitchen was a knock-about, panel

quiz show. 'Smartarse challenge.' In full on close-up Chicken saw that on the invited panel tonight was Harry Steadford.
'Shit,' whispered Chicken. He'd shared a stage with Harry no more than a few months before in North London. Harry was now pulling faces, making topical wisecracks and generally 'wowing' in the land of television. The well paid world of the biggest stage. Harry was good and even the other panellists were struggling to find room to breathe in the rat-a-tat comedy onslaught. 'Nice,' said Chicken dejectedly and turned the TV off.

At that very moment in a bedsit a hundred or so miles away a twenty three year old heckler from hell was being born. He twitched and cried out in his sleep and then sat bolt upright in his bed. The sheets were in a lump on his chest and he began to throttle them. Utter humiliation, embarrassment and shame were wrapped around him like a boa constrictor. He began to cry real tears. How had it happened? Why had it happened? What exactly HAD happened? That very night he had made his first and last appearance at an open mic slot of a local comedy club. He'd never before known reality to be so far from the fantasy. Always the one to make the hilarious remark at work and amongst his friends in the pub Danny thought that he knew his destiny - it was to be a comedy God. His racks of comedy dvds had shown him just how easy it was.

He'd planned it for months, found a club that let performers try out, certain in his mind that fame was just a case of them out there seeing how brilliant he was. Naively he'd even invited some friends to his debut. He didn't need an act as such or jokes as he had his personality.
He watched as the opening act, a fat man with a guitar had got the place chuckling although to Danny, having to rely on songs with funny lyrics was a bit clichéd. When the first guy

had finished the compere a cheery older man named Malcolm introduced him by saying,
'Here's a new one. Not sure what he's like. Might be good, might be shit.' He shrugged, 'Here he is. Danny.'
He'd taken the mic with a few scattered thoughts on his interesting day at the office knowing that he could easily ad-lb a whole set around that fertile ground. He'd seen so many famous comedians do it. Get them laughing and then gently string it out, keep jabbing them in the ribs. Don't forget to wait for them to stop laughing before you say your next bit he reminded himself.

It was the silence that had first unnerved him. The strangeness of standing on a low level stage, knowing that there were people in front of him, hearing what he was saying but not laughing. There was nothing coming back to him but excruciating quiet punctured by the odd cough. He stumbled on.
'And then Colin, Colin the tall one asked ME to un-jam the photocopier? I mean, like, yeah, right!'
He waited. No laughter. And then the shouts started.
'You're not funny,' and 'Get off'. Confused he lost his thread and in fact every thought he'd ever had fled his mind. He couldn't answer, he had no language anymore. Emboldened and sensing a kill the shouters got louder. 'Get the fuck off you twat.' Something small bounced off his face, he looked at the floor and saw that he'd been hit by a peanut. That got a laugh, and suddenly he was blinking in a wave of salty hailstones. He blinked in realisation that he was beaten.
'It's ok, I'm going,' he said quietly into the mic. It elicited the loudest roar of the evening. He jumped from the stage, ran to the back of the club and out onto the street. Now he was punching his pillow in rage. He was never, ever, ever going to do that again. Ever.
He got up from his mangled bedding hoping to ease his tortured mind. Pacing in a fever of pain he turned on the TV to be greeted by the gurning face of a new comedian called

Harry Steadford on some stupid quiz show. Sure, they were laughing – ho bloody ho.

'And you can fuck off too,' he screamed at the screen.

He stopped short of the rock 'n' roll posturing of putting his foot through the screen though. He was angry and hurt, but revenge on inanimate objects had never been any satisfaction to Danny. Human inflicted pain required human payback.

TWO

The computer whirred into life and Chicken slurped tea as it loaded the programs that were the tools of his trade. It was another harsh morning so once again he was a freelance graphic designer, it was how ninety-eight percent of his meagre income was generated. During the day in his kitchen-come office he played with his Apple Mac manipulating images and fonts to be used in adverts on book covers and in brochures. It was a job he'd trained for, he was good at and he hated. Chicken didn't think of himself as a skilled Mac operator and designer who dabbled in comedy some evenings, he thought of himself as a comedian funding his mortgage until he got his break.

His wife Laura, who was even then jiggling along on the Northern Line on her way to her office, didn't quite see it that way. She was the Marketing Manager of the large legal firm, Steel and Caskett and it had taken some years of mind numbing graft to attain that position. She was used to meeting high expectations and she was also used to meeting highly successful people. She didn't mind Chicken being arty but the rub for her was that for him to make more money he'd have to really concentrate on his designing. Instead of ringing round trying to find gigs he'd have to call more design studios for jobs. He'd have to spend time developing work contacts not spend hours writing jokes or in front of the lounge mirror rehearsing. He'd have to stop staying out late at comedy clubs so that he wasn't too tired to start proper work early the next day. In short, Laura felt that if they were ever going to get the kitchen extension of her dreams he would have to stop wasting his time. If he could get on TV of course then maybe that would all fall into place, but it had been six and a half years now and it hadn't happened yet.

The other secret that Laura had never been cruel enough to share was that she didn't think Chicken was funny. On a

personal basis he made her laugh sometimes, but his act? She'd only seen it once in a half empty club above a dangerous pub but that had been enough. Not to her taste, not her cup of tea. She'd heard others in the audience laughing and looked around mystified. Afterwards she'd avoided comment until pressed. Nodding vigorously and smiling slightly,
'Really different,' was all she'd been able to come up with.

Caravans were a pet hate, along with cardigans and sandals worn over socks. He hated looking at the travelling sheds as much as he hated being trapped behind them on dusty bank-holiday clogged roads. Chicken looked at his screen, a picture of a caravan to be dropped into a flyer and some uninspiring text to be made irresistible by his genius design. He sighed and moved instead to his emails and began trawling through his comedy folder. Promoters hardly ever answered emails and sure enough they hadn't today. He checked his calendar. No gigs booked for another week, three in for the next month and none after that. He toggled to the caravan image and then quickly to his document of comedy ideas. He had to rewrite some of his act and now was the best time to do it, while it was fresh, while the audience reaction was still stored in his memory.
An email pinged in and he dutifully checked it with that tiny burst of expectation that never left him. It was Duncan at the design studio asking when they were going to see the 'Travel Future' caravan flyer, which was already a week overdue. Chicken scratched his chin, there had to be a joke or two in that. Somewhere.
In his inbox an unopened message was glaring at him and had been for a week now. Every day it seemed to be a deeper shade of bold. He hadn't quite been able to delete it but he didn't want to read it either. Some weeks before Laura had excitedly given Chicken's details to a friend of hers who ran a full service advertising agency called 'Zingtastic' about a full-time position as an in-house

designer. Inwardly Chicken had groaned like a cow entering an abattoir. In-house and full-time as in a 'proper job', in an office with a steady income, that would be answerable to a boss and with full performance reviews and corporate bullshit. The awaiting email was probably about an interview. Especially as the subject line said 'interview'. There was a chance of course that it was to say that he wasn't getting an interview, but the irresistible force known as Laura had been involved so it was unlikely.

Thinking of her husband, and specifically subtle strategies for his career development that didn't involve a high-voltage cattle prod, Laura got off the tube in a bit of a daze. As the doors closed behind her she suddenly realised that she'd left her shiny, professional, look-at-me-I'm-important black leather briefcase behind. It was a present she'd bought herself, Chicken could never have afforded it, or even known what to buy, and it now contained some sensitive work documents. She turned quickly, panic in her throat as the train pulled away. She let out a cry of anguish only to be met by the smiling handsome face of Thomas from the office.
'You left this,' he said holding up her briefcase.
'God, thank you,' she snatched it eagerly from him, and then embarrassed by her loss of cool added, 'I never saw you on the train?'
He was still smiling.
'I was sitting across from you reading. You seemed lost in thought so I didn't like to interrupt. I saw you get up and leave your case though. It was my chance to be a dashing knight.' He smiled yet again. He certainly had nice teeth and in that moment, perhaps enhanced by her relief, he certainly looked like a hero to Laura. They began to walk through the crush towards the exit.
'Gosh, I owe you one Thomas.'
'Nonsense, Laura. It was nothing.' Thomas, the modest, polite, well-spoken hero knight. With perfect teeth. They climbed out into the dust and bustle of the street. As they

walked Laura noticed his shoes, expensive hand-made brogues. Chicken's ratty trainers came to mind. Thomas' cuff-links flashed as they poked from the sleeves of his nicely cut suit. Laura didn't have much to do with him at work, but she knew he was a bit of a high-flyer.

'Funny that I haven't seen you on the tube before,' she said.

'Well I recently bought a flat in town, you know since I made Partner, so my journey is a bit different during the week now.'

'Partner? I'm sorry I hadn't realised.' She was making an instant mental calculation.

'Yes,' said Thomas 'and it's good to be out of the main house anyway while the builders are there.'

'Builders?'

'Yes, bit of a kitchen extension in the barn conversion.'

'Nice,' she managed to whisper, her heart a flutter.

Matty Carlo, Morgan's booking agent and almost manager was on the phone trying to make Morgan understand how important this mini-tour was for everyone and as his agent that certainly included him. Matty had been dealing with artistes for long enough to know that not all good news was taken as such by the fragile egos that he managed. Dancers, singers and especially comedians - it made no difference. A sensitive artiste (and they were all sensitive) could see criticism in things that were said, things that were not said, things that were not even said but thought, or imagined to have been thought. Any comedian could stand in front of a crowd of a hundred laughing people and pick out the one person with a poker face then decide that it had been a bad gig. An incident like that could leave a funny-man traumatised for weeks.

Matty referred to his role as 'managing' because he didn't like to use the term 'handling' due to its obviously smutty connotations, although in truth he had handled a couple of clients over the years. Morgan was not one of the performers that he had handled, nor would he want to, but he didn't mind managing him for now. Morgan was a potential, a slow burner that might ignite and turn into a very lucrative name, but at the moment he was just hard work. The main job of being an agent was finding work for the clients of course and Matty was very good at that, but he had always thought that his prime skill was in cosseting. It was the ability to not only make the artiste feel like they were the only one on his books, a list that actually contained over twenty entertainers, but that they were the only people in the world. There were a few simple ground rules to stick as an agent such as never inciting professional jealousy by praising some other performer, never mentioning how well another client was doing and never letting the artiste know that you hadn't been thinking about them every waking moment.

Finding gigs for Morgan was easy, they pretty much found themselves, he was known and trusted on the circuit. The problem for Matty was moving him up to the next level, to the point where he would be recognised by the general public and the work and money would flow. The one advert that he'd already got for him wasn't going to be enough, but it was a start.

'Morgan, you've got to do the tour.'
'It's not a tour, it's four gigs.'
'It's a mini-tour.'
'In the North?'
'Yes, it's the North, but it's not those terrible Northern working men's clubs that you hear so much about from the old timers. These are proper alternative comedy venues.
'No one says alternative anymore Matty. That was the eighties. And don't tell me what the clubs are like, I know them all. I've played them all, year after year and I'm sick of them.'
'These are good clubs Morgan and the main thing is that at one of these gigs, and I stress again we don't know which one, the TV people are going to be there specifically to

check you out. That's right Upchuck Productions are sending two of their best, all the way up there to see you in action.'

Morgan was still in bed, phone in one hand beer in the other. 'Why can't they come to my gig tonight here in Shepherd's Bush? It's easier for everyone.'

Matty was trying to be patient but it could be frustrating, some of his clients could be very thick. It was as if they wanted to hurt their own careers. His frustration stemmed from his altruistic desire to see the very best opportunities develop for his people. It had absolutely nothing to do with his selfish need to milk more money from bigger promoters.

'They want to see how you play across the country Morgan, son. Out of your comfort zone. They don't want to invest all that money in a TV show if you haven't got universal appeal. They don't want you if you're too London-centric.'

'Up North?'

'Yes, up North. Come on, you have to trust me. Who got you the yoghurt commercial eh? Your profile has been up there since that aired.'

'But you know I've lost my driving licence Matty and they don't have the tube up there.'

'What is your problem Morgan? Don't you want to be a TV star? This could be huge for you. Get a train or get one of your mates to drive you.'

Morgan fully intended to do the tour, mini or not, it was just that he was enjoying being courted. Ever since he'd done the advert on TV life had been pretty sweet. Calls, emails and an agent who could actually find him work.

'Yes, well as it happens I'm working on a driver. He's got a car, and I won't even need to pay him.'

'What do you mean Morgan? Is he reliable?'

'Oh yes, this guy will work for a few open spots on the same bill. Way, way down the bill.'

Breezing into her functionally modern office with something of a spring in her step Laura casually threw a 'Hi' in

Elizabeth's direction, who was already at her keyboard rattling away like a witch with a box of bones. Elizabeth was Laura's PA, marketing assistant and marketing planner. In fact Elizabeth was Laura's whole department. She looked up with a beaming smile.
'So how did it go?'
'How did what go?'
'With Chicken? His gig last night?'
'Oh that. Fine. I think.' Elizabeth didn't notice Laura's lack of enthusiasm. She pressed on with genuine interest.
'He's here on the internet.' She was actually excited.
'Unfortunately, it's not a review though.' She began to read aloud, while Laura fussed around her own desk without even glancing at Elizabeth's screen.
'The Dodgy Club, Tonight's Comedy Mayhem, they mean last night obviously, International headliner Morgan supported by a chicken.'
Laura looked up.
'A chicken? That figures.'
'God, it's so cool though. You must be so proud, I mean he's so brave. I could never do that, stand up in front of people. What if they don't laugh, I mean how embarrassing would that be? He could be famous one day.'
Laura stared at Elizabeth for a few seconds, a quizzical expression on her face like a dog listening to a person talking about science. She snapped out of it and placed her gleaming bag on her desk to open its heavy brass catches.
'Elizabeth, do you know that guy Thomas in corporate?'
'Thomas Dalfin? Yes, a little bit. Lovely guy. Why?'
'Dalfin. Right. He rescued my bag. I left it on the train this morning.'
'Woah, that was lucky.'
'Very.' A tastefully understated thank you email was already forming in her mind.
'He was made a Partner recently,' continued Elizabeth.
'Yes, he mentioned it.'

'He used to be a bit frosty, bit work obsessed, but he seems much happier since his divorce last year.' She clacked away at the computer. 'So, anyway I'm trying to search but I can't find your husband's next gig? Where is it?'
Laura was standing with her hand on her bag. 'Do you know where Chicken's next comedy show is? We could go along maybe?' Laura blinked.
'Divorce?' she said.

He vainly checked his emails again, moved the picture of the caravan from one folder to another and decided it was time for a break. The travel job wasn't getting done, he just couldn't concentrate. He stood and walked through to the small lounge. From the bookcase he picked up the unplugged microphone, closed his eyes and imagined an audience. Not any individuals in the crowd, just a general mass of people which is how they always appeared to him. He practiced his walk out onto centre stage, the confident saunter that didn't give anyone a chance to think he didn't know what he was doing. Every detail counts, he thought. Don't show any gaps in your armour. They make their minds up before you even open your mouth. All good advice someone had given him back when he used to wander onstage like he was lost and not sure he should be there.
'Hello,' he boomed, 'thank you, it's great to be here.' Being a comedian who has just been introduced to the audience as Chicken, which was both his stage and street name, his first couple of self effacing minutes were always pretty much taken care of. Chicken now ran through his whole set adding some extra bits and dropping a couple of the jokes that hadn't gone down well the night before. He knew that now he'd lost confidence in those lines they'd never work for him again.
When he was just starting out Chicken had been told by a seasoned pro about what was called the tricycle of comedy, meaning that there were three main elements, or supporting wheels, to stand-up comedy. It was a phrase that Chicken

had knowingly used for a while until he discovered that it was a fantasy invention and no one knew what he was talking about. Still, the logic was sound and it had served to let him understand how a performance was structured.

The three parts were firstly content matter, meaning the subjects that you choose to talk about. By and large single comedians tended to talk about dates and older ones how funny it was having children. Pick the wrong subject for that night's audience and you were dead. Sometimes bawdy sexual references went down a storm on stag nights and sometimes the same incest jokes fell flat in the church hall.

The second element of the performance was comedy style in terms of whether the material was made into jokes and one liners that streamed out like foam from a fire-fighter's hose bathing the adoring masses in jollity, or if instead the comedy was wrapped in linked stories and personal observations. There were a lot of styles to choose from, sometimes it was nonsense simply spewed forth from a man wearing a kilt round his chest and a bucket on his head. A surrealist It was a matter of personal taste.

The third, and by far the most important factor in the success or failure of a routine was delivery, which was tied up with style but was more about how confident and assured the performer was. This was by a long, long way the most important part of the whole recipe. Bad jokes could be made funny by a funny comedian, a disjointed style could be made hilarious, but a set of good jokes and a great story could be killed by a jittery performer. Unfortunately vital as it was it was the part of the act that could only be honed in front of live audiences. Rehearsal could help you make things slick but timing and total confidence could only be gained through hundreds and hundreds of gigs. It was the reason that so many aspiring new-comers were willing to travel far and wide to get their shot in front of abusive drunks. It was on the job training of the most brutal kind.

Like the majority of the current performers on the circuit Chicken didn't really tell jokes, not in the traditional sense of, 'a man goes into a pub' or 'there was an Englishman, Irishman and another racial stereotype.' There were some circuit comedians who were closer to that style whose whole act was a string of one liners, one after another like a machine gun, but Chicken didn't do that, his memory wasn't that good. Chicken wrote all of his own material but rarely wrote it down. One of the unwritten rules of circuit comedy was that you didn't steal other people's jokes, and Chicken stuck to that. There was nothing worse than hearing someone else tell a joke you'd thought up, especially if they got a better laugh than you did. Chicken told personal observational stories that had punch lines. They were still jokes, but they needed a context, they didn't stand alone. They were exaggerated and embellished tales for the purpose of comedy but they all had a starting point in something that had happened to him. Or had happened to someone that he knew. Or he'd seen or heard about happening to someone else. Or he thought might have happened somewhere to someone. Verification didn't come into it, it was not intended to be reliable journalism or social commentary it was just comedy. Often when he was introduced to a new person at a social gathering and grandly mentioned that he was a comedian the inevitable response was 'Really? Tell us a joke.' to which his always disappointing reply before the stranger turned away was, 'I don't tell jokes. I'm not that kind of comedian.' This was a much better outcome than the other knee-jerk reaction from delighted new friends who might say, 'I know a great joke that you can use...'

On the well worn lounge carpet, in front of the imaginary crowd, he tried a new section on buying enough pain killers to commit suicide, stopped, changed some words, and re-worked it. It made him giggle which was a good sign, and he could also see avenues where it might be developed into a bigger piece.

He never rehearsed his final joke. It had been the same one for about 4 years now and it had never let him down. He was bored with it really, but he didn't dare drop a winner like that.

He paced up and down a little bit, trying to visualise the whole act as a movie then started all over again.

'Hello. Thank you, it's great to be here.' It was a difficult balance, rehearsing enough so that the words were second nature and couldn't be forgotten, but not overdoing it so they became tired and limp. The aim was to have it nailed down so it never went astray but loose enough that it came across as new and spontaneous. He didn't write down his act anymore, because he'd read that you shouldn't. A comedy set should never sound like a script. That's what he'd read. It was good to jot down ideas though and Chicken often wrote down headlines if he had a new part of the act to remember.

He ran through his act one more time in the mounting, oppressive silence of the lounge. Without the live audience there was only so much he could do. That was the curse of the comedian, it was only really comedy when other people laughed. You could practice the drums until you had it down perfectly and your neighbours had killed themselves, but telling jokes took interaction. Suddenly feeling empty and spent he sat down on the couch. The previous night's failed jokes began to take on a bigger profile in his memory than his laughs. Were there any laughs? Where were the gigs? Where was the groundswell of support? Why was it still such a struggle just to find a stage? Too much competition, too many comedians? Too many comedians who were funnier than him?

Back at his computer he'd had another email from Dunc. 'Listen, forget the caravan job, the client doesn't need it now.' He knew what that really meant, Dunc was telling him that they'd run out of patience with his failure to deliver and gone with someone else. A bad result. He slumped his head onto the desk as tiredness overtook him.

When Laura came home she found Chicken blinking and dazed, an incriminating sleeve impression stamped in his face.
'Oh. Hi,' he said obviously trying to fill in some gaps. His eyes were red. She looked quickly around the kitchen, taking in the breakfast dishes still on the table.
'I'm going for a run tonight,' she said. 'Have you done any food?'
He shook his head and she moved on through to get changed.
'There's a box of After Eight mints in the cupboard though,' he shouted after her.
'Oh, by the way,' she shouted even louder down the stairs, 'I spoke to Katy at Zingtastic today. Well done on getting the interview. You'll have to do some preparation.'

As she wearily climbed the stairs Laura's work phone bleeped at her. She was reluctant to read the text fearing an issue that would call for her attention and prevent her from going running. If she ever needed the pavement pounding relief of aggression it was tonight. She read the phone screen, at first frowning, then smiling broadly before staring at the phone thoughtfully. The message said, 'I sincerely hope you didn't leave your bag on the tube tonight! Thomas.' No text speak or appalling grammar, no childish smilie, not from Thomas the solicitor – true senior partner material.

Chicken paced the kitchen and began moaning aloud about the fact that nobody ever rang him back. Nobody. Ever. Rang. Him. BACK. No wonder his break just wouldn't come. No wonder he was forced to beg for gigs and constantly badger club owners. At Chicken's level there weren't any

agents to do any of the grunt work of listening to promoters grunting on the phone. Before an agent would take you on you had to have a constant stream of paying work. Agents were for successful acts, an irony that was not lost on any of those struggling to jump onto the bottom rung.
In the hidden hierarchy of low-level comedy Chicken was not actually at the bottom of the pit, although to the untrained eye it would be hard to see any difference. The lowest level was inhabited by the new acts who would take open spots wherever they could find them. That meant they didn't get billing, didn't get paid and usually didn't get laughs. For the opens it was a slog of two or three years of hard work before they could establish a big enough reputation to warrant being treated as a 20 minute middle spot. The early days involved a lot of gong shows which were little more than comedian baiting opportunities for vicious hecklers. After 3 years if they were still alive then they could move into the realms of sometimes getting paid a few quid 'for petrol'. Chicken was slightly above that now, he never worked for nothing, but he didn't work much.

The mobile phone next to the computer burst into life flashing and singing at a recognised number. He had first bumped into Morgan a few years before while he, Chicken, had still been doing the ten minute open spots. Morgan was already a professional and a respected headliner and Chicken had asked a lot of questions flattering the more experienced comedian. They had become friends but only in the very rare context of gigs where they were both appearing.

'Hi Morgan.'
'Something big mate. Chicken, do you want to go on a mini northern tour with me next week?'
'Um, maybe,' his heart was thumping with excitement. A tour!

'Thursday to Sunday. Hull, Bridlington, Scarborough and York. York's always a great gig.'
'So what's the deal exactly?' he was trying to sound cool and unimpressed.
'Well, I'm headlining but I'm sure we can get you some open spots. I'll pay for the petrol. I've got some mates up there we can stay with but we might need a B&B which I'll pay for.'
Chicken was suddenly cooler and less impressed.
'Right. I'm the driver?'
'A driver, WITH open spots. If I can swing it.'
'Right.'
'It's all experience Chicken. Remember, no gig ever makes you a worse comedian mate.'
'Yeah, but it's two days off work.'
'Okay? Are you busy?'
'Always busy.'
'At one of the gigs, and I don't know which one yet, but there will be some TV people. Producers.'
'To see you?'
'Well, yes of course me, they've never heard of you but you could change all that.'
'I'm not sure Morgan, it's short notice.'
'I know. Ok well look, I've got to get something sorted with someone because as you know I lost my licence, so if you don't want to do it...'
'I'll do it.'
'You sure?'
'Absolutely.' Chicken was observing the comedians credo, commit totally because you can always cancel at the last minute even if it leaves someone else in the shit.

THREE

Three days after his open spot humiliation, still smarting with the pain of rejection that was alive in his very skin, Danny, the failed one time only, and never again comedian was standing at the photocopier at work. On sober reflection, not that he'd been drunk, his open spot had become an open sore. As a young boy Danny's mother had once sent him to school in a pair of sandals and socks. Sandals weren't cool that year, or any year for that matter and the ridicule he had faced from the boys and girls in the playground had had a deep impact on him. He'd cried for days thinking that his young life could never recover, that he had lost the respect and support of his friends, that it was over for him before it had really begun. It had been very bad, but this was much worse.

The photocopier whirred on and would soon jam, as surely as sadness follows happiness. This was his destiny now, office drudgery. His entire work life wasn't actually spent standing at photocopiers and printers, it just felt that way. The planned escape into live performance and adulation followed quickly by sell out tours, TV shows, DVDs then blockbuster Hollywood comedy films had been cruelly taken from him. His whole future had been ripped away by the cruelty of an uneducated, ignorant and spectacularly ugly mob.

Out of the corner of his brimming eye, Danny saw a colleague approaching. It was Jonathan one of those whom he had stupidly invited along to be a witness to his downfall and therefore one of the several people that he'd been trying to avoid. In a strange manic excitement and with the total belief that he would be an incredible success Danny had told a lot of people about his aspirations and unfortunately some of them had taken him at his word. He'd thought that he was giving them a gift, the chance for them to say that they were there for his first ever public performance. It had backfired and it had crossed his mind that the only way he was going to be able to move on with his life was to either get a new job in a different town, or kill them all.

'So, Danny.' He was painfully cheerful. What did that mean? Who speaks cheerfully to a leper? 'Some of us are going out to another comedy club on Friday, I was wondering if you wanted to come along?'

Danny turned and scrutinised Jon. Was he taking the piss? Was this just a way of twisting the knife? Casual cruelty wasn't really Jon's style at all but perhaps he'd been put up to it by the others. Jon broke the uncomfortable silence. 'Well I know you like comedy, and there are loads of us going. You're welcome.'

Danny looked closely into Jon's eyes trying to gauge the subtext of this invite. How on earth could Jon not understand how agonising it would be for him to set foot in a comedy club? Was it possible that to Jon it simply wasn't a big deal? Impossible. The photocopier made the paper-jam, clunk and stop noise that usually made Danny's heart sink, but there was no deeper pit for his heart to drop into and he now welcomed the distraction. He turned away from Jon so that he could pull open doors, pull out drawers and try to read cryptic messages on the tiny screen. He heard Jon say, 'well like I said you're welcome to join us,' before moving away and Danny grunted an unintelligible,

'yauuahg', that meant, are you off your fucking head? You'll never see me in the sweaty confines of a comedy club ever again. You moron, weren't you there? Didn't you see and hear what happened to me?

The photocopier screen was scrolling a message that said, low quality output. Danny looked over his shoulder. He'd never seen that message before. Was the copier making a judgement, or had someone programmed it to say that? Even he could recognise the paranoia in that thought. He shook his head. He had to get a grip. Perhaps it would be better to get away this weekend, get out of town, right away, up north to his sister's maybe.

In the almost empty coffee shop the tables overflowing with the detritus of the expensive simple mixtures of milk, water and coffee beans, Davis a young comedy promoter of enormous self delusion was at the counter explaining a thing or two about the intricacies of running comedy nights to the young guy behind the counter.
'Understand this my friend, I run these comedy nights for one reason and one reason only. To make money. I don't even like comedy anymore. Sick of it. Had my day, winner of the North East Comedian of the Month regional heats, went down to London, lost to a comedy plate spinner. I mean in this day and age? Plate spinning? Mental. Anyway I'm sick to death of comedy but there are a good number of punters that do like a cheap night out – so that's what I give them. Not all promoters do make money mind, because they are the idiots and they give the profits back to the comedians. I don't do that. I book good headline acts which I pay for and the rest of them get nothing and they're glad to get it. They love being on the same bill and they think that one day they're going to be rich and famous. Idiots.'
He took a deep breath. The guy behind the counter nodded while his hand mechanically polished away at the small square of clean counter-top. He looked beyond bored, he looked, bovine. However, Davis carried on talking because he was not the sort of person to be aware of how another human is reacting. Had he been aware he was also not the sort of person to have the slightest care anyway.
'Take this coming weekend, Saturday night, I've got this comedian Morgan coming up – you've seen him on the yoghurt ad? Chucks yoghurt over a nun?' Counter-guy nodded and continued wordlessly polishing. 'I don't like him myself but I don't care whether he's any good or not, people want to see him that's all I care about. We'll have a packed house, I get a cut from the bar for bringing in punters and the

gate money is mine. I'll do alright out of it, bung him a couple of quid and there you go. So, anyway can I put this poster in the window? I'll get you a couple of free tickets?'
The counterman frowned, 'Free tickets for what?'

The old and trusty, crusty, rusty Mitsubishi edged slowly away, struggling to achieve the escape velocity needed to break free of Greater London's gravitational pull. Chicken hadn't mentioned to Morgan that anything over 60 miles per hour would overheat the car which functioned on half a radiator that was more leak fixing filler than anything else. When he'd said that they would be keeping it at ninety he'd meant degrees centigrade not speed. Heat and up-hills were a chore for the Mitsy, and of course Chicken had often noted that there were far more climbs than descents in any journey – both ways. Rain could also be a problem. Wet conditions often saw the old car slow down to a spluttering crawl – something to do with the electrics, which Chicken had neither the knowledge nor finances to remedy. Instead, for every journey his eyes flicked nervously from temperature gauge to speedometer, from hilly horizons to possible rain clouds.
On-board weight was also a concern for the Mitsy but thankfully there wasn't much luggage to carry on the trip, which was one of the advantages of being a comedian not a musician. No guitars, no amps, no drums to lug around, it was always the venue's responsibility to have a pa system and microphone. For Morgan and Chicken there were no props either, no ventriloquist dolls or dubious magic tricks, for them it was the traditional simplistic beauty of walking out to a microphone and talking for entertainment. Although they had no stage props Morgan did have stage clothes stuffed into a holdall that were indistinguishable from his everyday tatty clobber. They were only 'stage' in that they were clean, or at least not visibly stained. Chicken just wore his day clothes on stage as part of his man of the people persona, stains and all.

Even though they had no instruments or drugs or groupies Chicken couldn't help feeling that the tour had a strong element of rock 'n' roll in the fact that he didn't know where he would be sleeping that night. He hadn't quizzed Morgan about the accommodation arrangements trusting that it would all work out and not wanting to appear fussy and amateurish. He was sure that it was part of the deal that Morgan would certainly have sorted out hotels or something. He did know about the gig though, which was in Hull on the east coast, a name that brought little more to mind than a vague whiff of rugby league. However, Morgan had filled him in on some interesting information about the place, but not the kind that you'd get from a tourist information centre. 'It's actually called Kingston-upon-hull,' he'd said, 'but don't get carried away. It doesn't have the exotic appeal of Kingston Jamaica or even the affluence and of Kingston in Surrey, it's a shit-hole. It's way out on its own. Geographically. It's a port town that owes everything to fish and cod liver oil. That says it all really. But don't get excited, its not like a pretty Cornish fishing village. It's a shit-hole. In fact the most impressive thing about Hull is the huge bridge that gets you out of there.'

They drove in silence until Morgan finished texting and then he looked across at his driver. Morgan had never been married but several of his ex-girlfriends had formed the basis of his material, as had the very status of being single.
'So how did your misses take the news of your world tour?' he asked. 'Your East of Eden tour. Your grim up North tour?'
'She was pretty cool.'
Actually, it was true, Chicken had been expecting some sort of explosive discussion, but it hadn't happened at all. He'd prepped the news by explaining that there were no graphic design jobs coming through until the following Monday, and then subtly dropped in the fact that it gave him the perfect window to do a few gigs in the north, the 'big thing' with

Morgan that he'd told her about, from Thursday to Sunday, where there would be genuine TV company representation and therefore the chance to become rich and famous. He'd pitched it as a unique and once in a lifetime opportunity and at the moment that he'd been waiting for the onslaught, the quiz on the sticky subject of whether he was getting paid but it didn't materialise. Laura had nodded and then, 'sounds great and good luck ' was about all she'd said. She'd only raised an eye-brow when he'd described it as 'work'.
In truth Chicken's trip solved a sensitive problem for Laura. She'd been invited to a big deal company dinner that weekend at a very posh restaurant, in celebration of some newly won business, along with several of the partners and senior partners. As her partner of course Chicken had been invited too and it had caused Laura quite a bit of anguish wondering how she could avoid taking him. It wasn't only because he would be bored, although that's the excuse that she tried to convince herself was her main altruistic motivation. She was trying to deny it but her inner voice knew the truth. Thomas, her newly found text, email and tube journey friend would be there and she simply could not sit impassively as he or in fact any of the other partners and their partners asked her partner what he did for a living. She could not listen to him say, comedian. It wasn't that she was ashamed, no, it was just that it was, well..., embarrassing. She even regretted letting the nature of his hobby slip to Elizabeth months before. It had been one morning when she had been moaning about Chicken getting in late and waking her, which she'd described under her breath as 'because of his comedy thing'. Elizabeth's eyes had widened and she'd seized on the comment quizzing her relentlessly for the details, inexplicably fascinated by the grimy world of amateur hour comedy. Laura hadn't realised that Elizabeth actually paid her own money in her own time to go to comedy nights. When she wasn't being an efficient and effective PA, making Laura's work life just a little bit easier, she was some kind of sick comedy groupie.

The silly tour had fallen into Laura's lap and her social conundrum could now be easily and painlessly resolved. She watched as he pathetically wheedled his way through his flimsy justification and smiled at his transparency. She heard the word 'work' and raised an eyebrow because she thought for a second that he was talking about her work. Her mind was already scanning through her wardrobe for what to wear to the dinner. She was thinking that she wouldn't even need to tell Chicken about the invite, why bother him, it wasn't as if it was important. There was the other thing too. The fact that there would be a spare seat next to her now.

On the door, which bore the scars of daring to close too early from time to time, was a badly designed and laser printed sign announcing, 'The Dive. Rip-roaring' Comedy Night. Tonight MORGAN – from the hilarious TV yogurt ads'. Just inside sitting at a small round table was a girl, whom Chicken was sure would be the promoter's girlfriend. Ticket girls always were. She looked up expectantly as Morgan and Chicken shuffled through.
'£6 please,' she said, roll of tickets at the ready.
'Comedians,' said Morgan. She nodded. It wasn't that she recognised him it was that she knew that no one would pretend to be a comedian if they weren't.
'Alright,' she said, 'James is around somewhere. Near the back. Outside smoking probably.' James was the promoter and compere. Chicken pushed on past the table in Morgan's wake.
'I'm a comedian too. On later. Before him,' he smiled.
'Whatever,' she wasn't even looking at him now.
'Yeah,' said Morgan turning to him. 'I just need to have a quick word with James. See if we can get you on for an open spot.'
'He doesn't know yet?'
'Don't worry, it'll be cool.'

You didn't ring him about it? You haven't asked him?'
'He won't mind.'

The growing nervousness that Chicken had been feeling about going on stage was now replaced by a huge fear that he might not even get a chance. He was too tense to say anything now and meekly followed the headliner through the thin crowd. It was too early for the pub to be full yet but people were coming in all the time.

Dry, flat roads had meant that they'd made good time in the Mitsy, and even had time to grab a Chinese meal a few doors down from The Dive.
As they'd driven in on the concrete highway Chicken had seen the bridge that Morgan had mentioned earlier and he had to admit that as far as big bridges went it was truly spectacular, a rival to San Francisco's Golden Gate, although this one spanning the muddy Humber. It almost seemed to form an enormous letter H for Hull or maybe Humber and he wondered if that had been deliberate on the part of the designers. If he'd had his laptop he could have looked it up on the internet, but thinking that made him think of work, and with a jolt he remembered that he'd done nothing at all about Zingtastic and the job that Laura was trying to set him up for. He forced thoughts of 'real' life out of his head and tried to concentrate on the life he was living as a touring comedian. He glanced again at the bridge, he was quite looking forward to crossing it but then realised that they were heading towards the centre of Hull and away from the bridge. Under Morgan's guidance they passed the exit without using it.

'So why aren't we going on there?' he said pointing back at the receding structure.
'Two reasons. One we aren't going to Grimsby so we don't need to and two it costs money.'

Laura was absolutely NOT contemplating an affair or anything like it. She liked Thomas, and the fact that she enjoyed talking to him, travelling to and from work with him, emailing him and texting him was because they were friends. That's exactly what she had been telling herself since they'd started exchanging views on classical music, interior design, wine and great places to spend a holiday. There was way too much at stake for any silliness.

Laura had achieved her career through very, very hard work and she wasn't about to jeopardise that for a few months of dalliance. And of course Thomas wouldn't be interested in that anyway. He was a Partner for God's sake, he was an extremely busy man, a serious man with corporate responsibilities and a personal code of ethics. And no wife. And really sexy eyes. And money.

Elizabeth meanwhile had been intrigued and overjoyed to hear about Chicken's northern tour and had said a very strange thing. Laura had just been mentioning how much effort it took to become a Partner and Elizabeth had snorted.
'But they couldn't do what your husband does.'
'What do you mean?'
'Well, all those bores over in corporate. How many of them could stand, alone, on a stage, in front of all those people and entertain them? Make them laugh?'
'Why would they want to? They have real jobs?'
'No, I mean they couldn't actually do it. All it takes to be a solicitor is study and hard work. But you can't learn comedy. You can't learn to have that bravery.'
'Are you getting comedy mixed up with skydiving or something Elizabeth?'
'Could you do it?' Laura had never really thought about whether she could try comedy. She'd done a fair number of powerpoint presentations in her time. She'd raised a few giggles too with some clever observations on stats.
'I wouldn't want to.'
'But could you?'

'Elizabeth, I wouldn't want to, and what's more I'm not sure why anybody would. Now, can we see how the newsletter campaign is doing?'
Laura's phone rang.
'Hi, it's Katy,' it was an easily recognisable voice, posh, intelligent and dripping with the sharpness that made her so successful. Katy was her friend who had her own 'wildly successful' marketing company, Zingtastic.
'Oh, hi.' She always liked to hear from Katy because it made her feel connected and in touch with the female pulse of the business world, and not merely a functioning cog.
'Listen Laura, just to get to the point, is your husband not interested in the job? That's fine if he isn't, it's just that they're telling me that we haven't heard back from him about the interview and it's next week. I know you said he was coming in but he needs to confirm. '
Laura took a deep breath and then breathed a light carefree laugh down the phone. 'Oh God no, he's certainly interested Katy, it's just that he's gone away for a few days. Lads thing, so I suppose he hasn't had a chance to contact you about it. But listen, just give me the details and you can be sure he'll be there. I guarantee it.'

The Dive was not a club in the traditional night-club sense, it was like most comedy clubs a large, high-ceilinged, once grand building that was now a slightly shabby pub. The build-up of thick brown paint over the woodwork probably took inches off the overall internal capacity of the place. The long bar against one wall was facing a slightly raised platform behind a waist-high fairly pointless balustrade for a separate tables area, which was now cleared to be used as a stage. The mic stand was there, but there was no back drop and the audience would be surrounding the stage on 3 sides.

They walked out to a small courtyard where sure enough James was smoking. A man of about thirty, dressed like an overgrown student, known for his astute marketing, tightness of pocket and a streak of unreliability to match any comedian's. He presented all his own shows as compere because he was of course a comedian who hadn't quite made it. It was his way to keep himself out there. Chicken knew him only from the telephone. In the past he'd been booked to do a 20 minute slot in one of his Midland clubs, but the show has been cancelled, James had forgotten to tell him and Chicken had driven over a sixty miles before he'd got a text from another comedian. 'Turn back. It's off'. James would not remember the incident, and Chicken wasn't about to remind him.

Morgan and James exchanged a few words about this comedian, that club and that promoter and then James said, 'Okay, I'll compere, I'll introduce the opening act, Sarge, then a break for drinks, then we've got an open spot. Then another break. Then I do a bit and then you.'

'Great,' said Morgan. Chicken kicked him in the back of the leg. 'Oh, yes. Can Chicken do an open too?' he gestured at Chicken. James looked as if he'd suddenly had a bad smell thrust under his nose as he assessed him.

'Two opens?' he looked at Morgan's impassive face and thought about the ramifications of annoying his headliner, the person who would probably be the only genuinely funny person of the night. 'Okay, why not? Two opens. We'll put him on after the other guy.'

Chicken felt relief, followed fast by fear and a need to go to the toilet.

The crowd grew steadily bigger and Chicken reasoned that there couldn't be too much to do in that part of Hull on a Thursday night. They sat near the back and he chatted with Morgan who was assessing and grading the crowd, looking for anyone who could possibly be from a TV company.

'What about that guy? Trendy bald fucker?' he asked nodding at a nearby table.

'You've got issues with bald, do you know that?'

'If I didn't have issues I wouldn't be a comedian.' Morgan was drinking a pint but Chicken dared not.
'I've got to get this TV thing.' he said mostly to himself. 'I can't do fucking Edinburgh this year. It's saturated. It cost me a fortune last year. Playing to ten twelve people in some back-room? I had to hire the room. I didn't earn anything. It was a nightmare. All in all I lost four grand on Edinburgh last year.' Chicken was wishing that he had four grand to lose. 'But people are scared. They don't dare NOT go to Edinburgh. They think everyone will think that they've dropped off the planet if they don't make it up there. Well fuck it. If I can get this TV thing they can fuck off.'
Chicken had noticed before that Morgan's profanity rose in direct relation to how close he was to going on stage. It was a sad truth though, nothing made drunken audiences laugh more than carefully aimed swearing.

Usually when he was waiting to go on Chicken was silently running through his material, but for some inexplicable reason he felt relaxed tonight. He'd visited the toilet and he felt calm internally and externally. His mouth wasn't even dry. Perhaps it was down to the journey with Morgan and the way it had made him feel like a proper comedian.
The young man who was going to do the open spot before Chicken's came over and introduced himself as Jim, a nervous and strangely earnest guy who looked as if he was probably no more than a year or two out of student-hood. Chicken immediately felt superior and that feeling did not change when eventually Jim took to the stage. He was all wrong. Wrong stance, wrong material, wrong lack of jokes. What was worse was that he started asking the audience why they weren't laughing. The crowd to their credit were patient, but only up to a point. They'd been primed by James in his introduction that Jim was new to comedy and for a while they seemed to bear that in mind. Morgan and Chicken looked at each other. The room began to get heavy with frustration until someone shouted from the back,

'What are you up to?' A slightly bizarre heckle that summed up the problem. Jim didn't know what he was doing. Fearing an ugly backlash, or worse someone asking for their money back, James brought the act to an end and taking the mic announced, 'Well that was bad.' It was an attempt to put himself on the same side as the punters. He had a few digs at Jim, who was still in the room and then with the words, 'Let's hope this one is better.', introduced Chicken.

Chicken walked confidently to the stage, he knew that he wasn't as bad as Jim and it made him feel great. As he hit his first couple of quick-fire one liners there was a noticeable lifting of the weight and a mass wave of relief swept through the room. Chicken was flying. Based on Jim's attempts they hadn't been expecting very much from the open spot, but Chicken did know what he was doing. He may have been languishing in an open spot, but in fact he wasn't new and he was able to flex all of his hard won experience. As his act ran on and his confidence grew and grew he enjoyed every second. Even the new stuff worked and when he reached his final joke he was sad to let it end.

'Thank you. You've been brilliant.' He shouted above the huge applause.

As he walked through the crowd a man in a shell-suit stopped him.

'That was great man.' He had the comb-over and the overly serious look of a possible nutter.

'Thanks.'

'No, I mean like you were funny. Really.' He was staring intently at Chicken as if this would be very surprising news. He leaned in a bit closer and Chicken couldn't help but lean away. 'You made me laugh.' he said as if giving some very precious news. Life saving news.

'Thanks,' said Chicken again and made his way to the sofa at the back of the room where Morgan was sitting. James was telling the audience that there would be a short break to get drinks before tonight's as-seen-on-TV headliner would be with them.

Chicken flopped down on the sofa next to Morgan who said, 'You must have enjoyed that.' He was smiling, but tensely, his own test still to come. Chicken tried to play it down. 'Yeah not bad,' but inside he was ecstatic. It had been worthwhile, the journey, the time off work, the whole thing. As the adrenaline of fear ebbed away to be replaced by the endorphin of joy he began to feel completely spent. And then a really sharp jolt of excitement hit him. What if the TV people were there? What if they'd witnessed his triumph?

Danny had fled his bed-sit and his office and work colleagues to give himself the boost of some fresh surroundings for a few days in the hope that by the time he went back he'd feel better. Maybe he'd have stopped thinking that the office equipment was ganging up on him because he'd been so terrible at his attempts to be a comedian. Maybe he would lose this powerful but unfocused desire for revenge against someone he couldn't name. Comedy watchers in general perhaps? Maybe he could stop shrieking in the night. However, he couldn't help thinking that although time heals all wounds a long weekend probably wasn't going to be enough to stitch-up the gaping hole in his psyche. It was supposed to damage a person when people laughed at you but no one ever mentioned how damaging it was to have people not laugh at you when you really, really wanted them to. He had filled his car with petrol and driven north to the outskirts of Scarborough where his sister Jane, her husband Brian, her three children and their collie dog all lived in a vision of domestic bliss. Close enough to the beach to walk the dog on it every day. Far enough from Scarborough to avoid the horrible bits and the holiday makers.

Danny sat and watched, with a comforting cup of coffee steaming in front of him, spiritually soothed as Jane busily prepared lunch. Nice. It was working, the distraction.

'On Saturday,' said Jane, 'we're all going to go out into Scarborough. We've got a baby sitter, so I'm glad you came up because you've given us an excuse to escape for the night.'

Danny felt a clenching inside and closed his eyes he just knew what was coming. It was like a computer guided homing missile about to hit. Why did fate do things like this? He hadn't told his sister why he'd come up at such short notice for the weekend, he'd only said that he needed a break. He hadn't said that he needed a total break from the echoes of his shame of comedy. 'I know how much you love comedy,' she continued, 'so Brian managed to get some tickets to a comedy club in town. Isn't that brill? There'll be us and a few of our other friends, NOT all couples by the way. Brian says that the main bloke is quite well known, he was on a yoghurt advert or something.'

'I can't go.' Jane stopped her kitchen table fussing. She looked devastated.

'Why? What's wrong?' He decided against spilling the failed comedian beans. It would be too painful to have to go through the whole thing with her. He'd hoped that he wouldn't even have to think about any of it for a few days, but here it was again. Haunting and taunting him.

'I just, I just don't really fancy it. I could baby sit while you all go.'

'We've already booked the baby sitter.'

'I'm not in the mood.'

'What is the matter with you? You love comedy Dan?' She was obviously very disappointed and starting to be concerned. Danny now started to feel guilty. It was true he'd fallen out of love with comedy, but he loved his sister and there was no reason for a bunch of cretins in a pathetic audience to make him, make her feel bad. 'Brian's really been looking forward to it too.' He sighed.

'Okay,' he blurted putting on a fake smile, 'we'll go.'

'No, really, if you don't want to…'

'I was kidding with you Jane. Of course I want to go. I mean, come on. You know me, I love comedy. Me. It's my best ever thing.'

He hugged her so that he could hide his expression, it was killing him to force the grin. Over her shoulder he stared at the calendar filled with dentist's appointments, dance lessons and school trips and started to rationalise. Maybe it would be better to face up to his demons than avoid them? That would be the manly thing to do. It was like getting back on a horse. After all he couldn't make it through the rest of his whole life without ever going to a comedy club. He frowned. Well, obviously plenty of people didn't even know that such things existed and still lived fulfilling lives, but for him it was something he just had to do. The Gods had followed him up the motorway and dropped this on his head so he had to get it over with and bite the bullet. Bite it, chew it and swallow the barbed-wire bullet of fun filled with acid poison.

After Morgan had finished his set, which Chicken was too wrapped up in re-living his own to notice much, like any professional who has done his job he was ready to leave. He had a very quick, money based discussion with James, then nipped off to the toilet leaving the promoter nodding at Chicken.

James patted Chicken on the shoulder.

'Good stuff by the way. Your set. Thanks. Well, I'll call you about other gigs. You're on my radar now.' Chicken knew that James's radar wasn't even turned on. It was an embarrassing conversation. Morgan had already been paid, in cash, but Chicken was getting nothing, even though both he and James knew that he'd been worth a few quid tonight. It was like they said, you don't get what you deserve, you get what you negotiate. It worked both ways though, in the past Chicken had been paid on nights when he hadn't been worth a cold kipper in the face.

It was too late now to call Laura, she'd be asleep, re-energising for the next day at work, still it would've been nice to share with her how fantastic it had been. Morgan still hadn't said where it was that they were staying but as they walked out into the Hull night and headed towards the car Chicken wondered if Morgan would congratulate him or pass comment on the strength of his performance. They stopped at the unmolested car and Morgan looked straight at him and asked, 'So, where are we staying Chicken?'

Later in the B&B that Morgan had booked they lay in a shared room in separate beds. Thank God for the separate beds thought Chicken. They had been sipping vodka from the bottle and Chicken was starting to come down from the euphoria of the gig. He listened to one side of Morgan's telephone conversation with Matty, his agent.
'So they weren't at that one? You know that now? So will they be at the Bridlington gig? Why don't you know? I know it's very late but this is show business Matty. It's rock 'n' roll. We've got drugs and hookers and everything here. Relax, we'll be there, but those TV pricks had better fucking be there Matty. As soon as they've seen the act I'm back to London.' He finished the call and Chicken thought that he'd gone to sleep. Neither of them had wanted to venture out into the strange place in search of very late nightlife. Chicken was glad because if Morgan had wanted to stir up some action the pressure to follow would have been intense.
'We bring them happiness,' Morgan said into the dark, presumably for Chicken's benefit. He was getting used to the little lessons that Morgan put his way and actually quite enjoyed them. It was Chicken's role to listen without interruption. 'All entertainment is distraction and distraction means you can forget for a while. That makes them happy because all happiness is a function of forgetting.' There was a glug noise as Morgan drank vodka. 'On a micro level it's forgetting about the pain in your foot or things that you

haven't done in the house, the money you need, the money you owe, the hurtful things that people have said to you.'
There was a silence and Chicken was about to answer when Morgan spoke again.
'On a macro level it's about forgetting the state of the world, the starving and the suffering, those that are fighting, dying, being tortured and abused. Right now, right this minute that's happening and if you can't forget about it you can't be happy.'
'I guess so.'
'Forget it all because it all turns to shit in the end.' Chicken recognised that phrase from Morgan's act, it was part of one of one of his routines, but he wasn't trying to be funny now. 'Muscle turns to man boobs. You can't escape.'
Chicken lay awake in the strange room staring into space waiting for Morgan's next instalment of wisdom, but it never came. He thought about Laura and suddenly about the job interview that she was setting up. A pang of guilt chilled his bones and he leaned over to the bedside table and got his own phone. He began silently texting. She wouldn't have her phone turned on now, but at least she could read a text from him in the morning. There were no messages from her.

But Chicken was wrong. Laura's phone was still on and buzzed to let her know that she had a message, she quickly peered at the screen in the gloom of the bedroom, and then sighed because it wasn't the message that she'd been hoping for.

FOUR

Chicken awoke to an insistent thumping sound and it took more than a few seconds to work out where he was. He took in the stained wallpaper and dark brown furniture. He looked over at the bulky form of his roommate who had not stirred. Someone was banging on the door and shouting, 'Check out is 10. Check out is 10.' He squinted at his watch it was 10:45.
He eased his way out of bed and stood painfully on the empty vodka bottle. He hopped round in a circle before he remembered that there was no en-suite bathroom, facilities were down the hall. He sat on the edge of the bed for a while until the thumping had stopped and he dared to venture out to toilet.
When he got back to the room Morgan still hadn't moved so Chicken shook him.
'Morgan. We've missed breakfast and we've got to get out.'
There was a muffled response.
'If I wanted to get up at the crack of dawn everyday I'd get a job.'
Chicken sat down again. Not much was left of the excitement of the previous night's performance. The room which he had only seen in the dark did not benefit from the harsh daylight. He had been secretly hoping that Morgan's budget would have run to a hotel and separate rooms but in the end he'd been glad just to have somewhere to lie down. As late as it was when they'd arrived before they'd been allowed to stumble into the room they had had to give a credit card to the nasty looking owner. I mean, thought Chicken, if you don't like letting people stay in your guesthouse why do it? Cash wasn't acceptable and Morgan couldn't find his card amongst his clutter so Chicken had handed his across instead. As it stood right now, Chicken had paid to take Morgan to a gig that Morgan had been paid for. He'd have to sort that out before Laura got a peek at the

card bill. He'd have to get the petrol money back too. It had been a pretty clear deal, they weren't supposed to be sharing the travel costs, it was Morgan's trip. A very slight whiff of 'what the hell am I doing? breezed through Chicken's mind but he pushed it away before it could take hold.
The thumping on the door started again.
'If you aren't out by 12 you get charged another night,' shouted the same voice as before.
'Right,' said Chicken pulling the covers off Morgan. 'we're definitely out of here.'

Emails were simply one of the tools of the trade for Laura. There would be no marketing without, emails, sms, powerpoint and excel. Emails were boring but necessary. Ho, hum another email meant another job to do. But something strange had happened, since becoming friends with Thomas Dalfin emails had somehow become exciting. Crazily she was checking her inbox every ten seconds, hoping for the bold lettering of his name. And the thing was that as important and busy as he was Thomas was finding time to email her. He worked in the next building to Laura and generally worked through lunch but they had been out for sandwiches a couple of times. For a man in such an important job he was fun.
Currently Laura was supposed to be organising a very big and important seminar on the tax implications of certain recent legislation. It was a chance to get together heavy hitters from the legal departments in the city and show them how clever and in-touch Steel and Caskett were. It was all useful positioning but she hated organising seminars, there were so many things that could go wrong and the mistakes were so visible. There were a lot of emails and powerpoint presentations and excel spreadsheets to send to people this morning, but Elizabeth could handle that while Laura spent some more time thinking about what she was going to wear to the Partner's dinner. She saw the tiny envelope icon, checked and was thrilled to see there was an email from

Thomas. She deliberately waited a few minutes tempting herself before thrillingly reading the message. 'Have you decided what you're wearing to the restaurant yet?' Uncanny. She'd been thinking about exactly that and here was his email. It was definitely a sign; they were tuned in and on the same page. True, it had been a bit of a joke between them this morning on the tube. (He got the train a few stops before her and she'd had to let one go before Thomas's had arrived.) He'd complimented her on her outfit as he always did and then playfully teased her that she wouldn't need to be so corporate when they went to the dinner.
She read a little further down the email and suddenly hit a sour note. 'So, will we get to meet your husband at the dinner?' She sighed. Oh yes, her husband. She hadn't heard from Chicken except the short text sent late last night. Obviously jabbed out with drunken fingers it said something about his great night. Good for him. Laura had not replied to that but she now replied to Thomas. 'No, he's away on business. I'm way too busy to be thinking about dresses Thomas – I've got a seminar to organise. So, what about you?'

She meant was he thinking about what to wear, but a reply pinged back almost instantly. 'No, haven't got a husband, I'm going on my own.' She hesitated for only a few seconds before answering again. 'Might be a bit boring, maybe we can keep each other company?' It was a long morning waiting for an answer to that one, a long uncomfortable time in which it was impossible to do anything except constantly refresh her inbox. In those torturously slow hours she imagined Thomas shocked and repulsed and forwarding her email to HR under the subject line, harassment. Eventually his name popped up and Laura anxiously clicked the click. 'Sorry, been in a meeting. Yes, what a good idea, maybe we can go for a drink beforehand?'

On the other side of the room Elizabeth meanwhile had been tapping away quietly at her own computer and suddenly sat bolt up-right in a state of obvious excitement.
'There's a review!' she said, 'Chicken has a review on the internet of his show last night in Hull. A place called The Dive. They have a website and there is a review.'
'Right.'
'Wow, only a couple of lines but listen. 'Blah, blah, blah Morgan and the newcomer Chicken showed a command of jokes and delivery that tells this reviewer he's not as new to this as he pretends. And there was that very funny twat joke.' She looked up from her screen beaming. 'Did you hear that?'
'Nice,' said Laura. 'a funny twat joke. I wonder if it was my twat?'
The smile was starting to edge from Elizabeth's face. 'I thought you'd be interested.'
'Elizabeth, it's all very fascinating, but I think we've got a conference to sort out. Am I right?'

Over the drone of the car Chicken said, 'I know it's naff to have readymade put-downs, but I really don't like hecklers. Trouble is, I don't think I'm confident enough to deal with them. I like to stick to my act, so that I don't forget where I am. I don't like being side-tracked.' Morgan nodded.
'The popular mythology surrounding the heinous act of heckling goes a bit like this. Silly heckler makes a semi-funny comment and the expert comedian responds with a very funny put-down that gets the crowd laughing at the heckler. The crowd are on the comedian's side and the beaten heckler is shamed into silence. But as we both know it rarely happens like that. The reality is usually an unintelligible, drunken, abusive tirade from the dark. It's ceaseless and it is only encouraged by the audience's disapproval. The comedian tries to get the better of the drunk, hits out with a few put-downs but the noise keeps coming back. The comedian can't get on with his well rehearsed and incredibly hilarious act. The crowd misses

out, Everyone loses except the heckler who's too drunk to know and would tell you that it's all part of the experience anyway,' he paused, 'But that's not to say that some comedians don't enjoy it. Some do base their entire act on heckling the audience but it works best when the crowd are sober enough and funny enough to add something themselves. I'm not a fan of it myself, but if you can come up with some good quick lines it can work out for you.'
'I know,' mumbled Chicken, 'I've seen it too, but like I say it's just this confidence thing, and my bad memory.'
'If you want I'll heckle you so you can get used to it.'
'No, no need, it's only...'
'GET OUT OF THE CAR. YOU'RE RUBBISH.'
'No really, you don't need...'
'YOU ARE COMPLETELY CRAP. STOP TRYING TO DRIVE.'
'This could get tedious.'
'THINK YOU'RE A DRIVER, YOU'RE USELESS.'
'Fuck off.'
Morgan at last smiled and nodded, 'Now you're getting it.'

Davis the promotor was sitting in his modest flat in front of his flashy lap-top where he did his best work. He saw himself as a professional networker of immense talent and the internet was his best friend. With Saturday's show coming up he was tinkering with his website and sending emails, drumming up business. He wanted a full house and he knew that wouldn't happen by accident, he needed the telly association of this guy Morgan. Gates had been slightly down recently and it was upsetting him. It wasn't his only cause of agitation though. Davis was feeling very pressured and it didn't help his usually frenetic personality. The problem was that he had a strong feeling that the 'Grand Night Out' comedy club that he'd founded, built and worked tirelessly to promote was about to bite him in the arse. Or more importantly in the wallet. A comedy club was a very intangible entity, very hard to contain or own. It wasn't really about the venue because that could change, it was much more about the crowd pulling reputation of the name that was important. The audience had to feel that whenever they turned up at that club they were going to have a great time. That's why Davis was always ready to pay for headliners even if they had to come up from London. Headliners never failed and they sent the audience home happy, and hopefully ready to come back the next week for more.

Amongst a number of enterprises, like his comedy school, Davis had been running a successful club at the Grand hotel in Scarborough for four years. During the dark days of winter when the East Coast deadened beyond its usual moribund state there was still a hard core of locals who needed fun and would take it where they could find it. The Grand Night Out had worked pretty well, bringing in drinkers for the hotel and keeping it alive, but there had recently been changes, a newly appointed manager seemed to have designs on the club himself. He'd already hinted to Davis that there didn't seem to be much involved in booking a few comedians and why were they letting Davis take the gate? For Davis the maths went like this: 150 punters through the door at £6 each was £900. You had to pay out £150 to £200 for a decent headliner, because he was the guy (and it usually was a guy) that everyone would remember. Then there was another £30 for some other comedian to open the show, and then a beginner or open spot for nothing in the middle. Tidy profit, all cash and it was worth it. Unlike some of the lazier promoters Davis usually put about £100 into marketing and promoting each show and it still left him earning money. In the early days Davis had also been able to convince the management to give him a cut of the bar takings, but not lately.

The danger was that if the new manager took the name 'Grand Night Out' to run it as his own club, and frankly how could Davis stop him, people would still come to the hotel and he, Davis, would miss out. He could try to move his club but he would probably lose his hard won regulars along the way. The truth was that there we no contracts or signed agreements at this end of show business. It was all down to trust, and of course absolutely no one could be trusted. Davis' main strength was that he knew where the comedians were, which ones were any good and how to get hold of them. He sighed. As a strength it wasn't very strong. The internet was full of agencies who would snatch any venues' arm off to get their acts on. All in all it was a worry to him, and when he was worried Davis sometimes did strange things.

Morgan and Chicken were sitting on the deserted beach at Bridlington. It was nearly midnight and getting cold as they drank from their cans looking exactly like the couple of tramps that they were only a heartbeat from being. Behind them, on the other side of the low level sea wall was the Seaton Hotel where they had performed that night at the 'Big Brid' comedy club. As usual 'club' was a slightly misleading description for the large airy, atmosphere free function room of the hotel that had been laid out with chairs and tables and a stage set up to one side. Weedy, the compere who fancied himself as an avant-garde man of comedy had been running films on a small overhead projector before the gig, their humorous subtleties passing over the top of most of the audience.

The crowd who numbered around 50 by the time the gig kicked off formed what almost passed for a private party. They were in a good mood but in Weedy's introductory phase of 'where are you from?' and 'who are you with?' it became apparent to Chicken who was standing at the back, that the whole audience knew each other. They were family and friends and Bridlington folk who liked to hang out together. And drink.

On the back of his previous night's triumph Chicken had gone on stage full of confidence, waiting for the inevitable 'good gig', but it just didn't happen. It wasn't bad, it wasn't a disaster, it just didn't work right and he couldn't put his finger on why. Perhaps he'd come across as too self assured and cocky? As if he didn't think he had to work for the laughs when he knew that actually you always had to work for them? As he walked off to limp and uninterested applause, a kind of, thank God that's over on to the next type of clapping, he was plunged into self-doubt and depression. How could exactly the same act as the night before have such a different reception?

Morgan on the other hand had been Morgan. Same act, same great reception. The Bridlington brothers, sisters, mums, dads and cousins had laughed and whooped their little lungs out. The only one in the room not laughing was Chicken which added to his feeling that it wasn't the audience, it was him.

After the gig Morgan and Chicken grabbed some cans and wandered out onto the beach where a few lads from the crowd were sitting. They gladly welcomed the exotic comedians into their little party, or at least Morgan who was as close to a celebrity as they had ever got that near to. They regarded Chicken with a certain pitying politeness. It didn't take long however before the disappointed locals realised that off stage was a different world, that the comedians weren't going to supply endless entertainment and they got bored. As they drifted away one of them mumbled something about why they weren't funny anymore and Morgan responded under his breath that he hadn't asked the stranger to do his job, if he had one.

After a while Morgan said, 'Well, the TV executives certainly weren't at that one.'

'How do you know?'

'They'd have stuck out humans in the chimps enclosure.' Chicken brightened a little. 'Ok, so on to the next one. Saturday night in Scarborough.'

'Unfortunately, yes, we have to go on.'

Chicken picked up a stone from the sand and threw it towards the sea which was too far away to see in the darkness.

'That felt bad for me tonight,' he said quietly, 'I actually felt like I was getting somewhere last night in Hull, but tonight...I don't know.'
'You did fine,' said Morgan. 'That's the way it goes. It's called regression to the mean.'
'Meaning?'
'You're on a learning curve, it takes seven years to become a comedian and you are on that curve. You are going to jump up, like last night, then you'll sink back to the curve the next night and it'll feel like you've lost ground. You'll make huge leaps and then you'll plateau. You just have to keep going and keep doing as many gigs as you can.'
'You never die do you? You're always on the money.'
Morgan snorted. 'Let me tell you about my recent corporate gig. Matty, my agent, rings me and says that he has a really plumb corporate gig at some architects' conference. It's about two grand for one gig, so I jump at it. I had to cancel the gig that I was going to do that night so that I could do it, mainly because I'm greedy and I thought it might open some doors for me.
Anyway, I get there and they want me to sit at the top table at this big fuck off dinner thing and when they've all eaten I'm to do about 45 minutes.' Morgan stopped to drink and gather strength.
'So the dinner was nice and then they get to my bit and the main guy says something like, 'We've never done this sort of thing before and sorry you're the guinea pigs, but here's a special treat. Not the usual industry expert but a comedian.' And so I stand up. I go hello, how are you tonight. Nothing. I go, my name's Morgan did you have a nice dinner? Nothing. I'm sweating now so I just go right into my routine. Nothing. People really close to me are shaking their heads and frowning. One or two get up and go. I get about fifteen minutes into it and I just say, 'Listen, I'm not so sure you're really enjoying this, so would you like me to stop and we'll just call it quits?' and they all clapped.'
'And you left?'

'Yep, walked out and as soon as I was out of sight I ran.' Then he looked hard at Chicken. 'But the worst thing was I didn't get paid, you know why? I should have done my 45 minutes. I could have done a terrible 45 and still been paid, but because I ran I lost it.'

Chicken laughed. 'I did a gig in Leicester about two months ago and there were only 5 people in the audience. Serious looking blokes. Turns out they were all fire-fighters and they'd been to a really bad fire that day and they weren't really up to laughing.'

'Why did they turn up at a comedy club?'

'I guess they had the tickets.'

'And you died on your arse?'

'There were 4 comedians on the bill and we all died on our arses.'

'Burned to death.'

'Yep. So why do we do it? Why would anybody want to put themselves through that?'

'I do it because it's my job. I'm a professional comedian and it's better than doing a proper job.'

'But all comedians want out don't they? As soon as they can they move into TV and if they can they do movies or whatever else they can. In fact anything but stand-up. I mean you want out too Morgan, you're desperate to get in front of these execs so you can land this TV show so you can leave these gigs behind.'

'Maybe you're right, but you know what I think? I think we'll sleep on the beach tonight. Have you ever been to Greece? It's the wild rock 'n' roll, student thing to do.'

'Yes, that sounds good. Rock 'n' roll hypothermia.'

'It really isn't that cold. We have the insulation of alcohol.'

'You do know that alcohol is the insulation that leads to people dying in the snow?'

'Snow? We're at the seaside. It's like the south of France. Honestly we could sleep on this beach.'

'No, you couldn't.' The voice had come from behind them and they turned and looked up to see a policeman, smiling down at them. He was obviously trying his friendly community policing stance at the moment, but his colleague who was standing further back was already glowering in 'bad-cop' mode. For a few seconds nothing was said until Morgan spoke.

'Officer, has anyone ever told you what lovely eyes you have?' Chicken giggled but it was a smart-arse crack too far for bad-cop. He bustled forward, his protective vest swelling over his chest, his hand on his truncheon.

'Come on, get up and get moving.'

'It's a public beach is it not? We were just enjoying the sea air, sir. I thought that was what beaches were for, lying down and looking at the sea. You should be promoting tourism. Why don't you sit down and join us?'

'It's not a drunk's doss house. This is your last chance to do as I'm telling you,' said the lawman, in his uncompromising Yorkshire whine.

Chicken was incredulous, why would Morgan want to start an argument with the cops? Unless of course his idea for accommodation was hoping for a warm night in the cells.

'Just get moving,' said the cop. Morgan sighed, knowing a tough crowd when he saw one and tiring of trying to bait them. They rose unsteadily and began to move slowly up the beach towards the hotel where they had performed earlier. The police watched them go, their crackling radios becoming fainter in the distance.

'So where are we staying tonight Morgan? I can't drive you know, especially now we've come to the attention of the authorities.'

'Don't sweat it. I booked it yesterday. We're at the hotel where the gig was. They do a B&B deal for visiting comedians.'

FIVE

'So, now we've paid for two nights of bed and breakfast and so far no breakfast.' They were in the car heading through the cloudy morning the short distance up the east coast.
'It's okay, we can get breakfast in Scarborough.'
'We've got a lot of hours to kill before the gig tonight.'
'We'll go on some rides.'
'Rides?'
'Yes, Scarborough is like Disneyland.'
'Is it?'
'Well, the southern part is. Disney with fish and chips. The North Bay is more serene and genteel. Some nice architecture, beach huts, stuff like that. Actually with some investment Scarborough could be the Brighton of the North. Only one thing stops it.'
'The climate?'
'Nope, the people who go there. Exclusively fat northerners with tattoos, rather than the skinny ones in Brighton. If Scarborough could harness the pink pound it could really move forward, but so far it hasn't happened.'
'Nice.'
'They'll never be able to stop them. Mind you, unbelievably there is a big surf scene in Scarborough. I think it's based on the bad weather and big waves. I think they'd like it to be the Newquay of the North. Of course Newquay wants to be the California of Britain, so that would make Scarborough the Malibu of North Yorkshire. But you know what's stopping it?'
'The people?'
'Damn right dude.'

When Laura woke in the half empty marital bed there was the initial surge of excitement that always accompanied Saturdays but it increased in volume when she remembered that tonight was the night of the meal. In fact, she thought of it as 'her' meal, arranged for and placed by fate before her.

As she kicked her feet gleefully across Chicken's side of the bed she had a sudden and completely unexpected pang of guilt. What was she guilty about? This was a company meal where she would be able to cement and enhance her 'Steel and Caskett' career prospects. She had only been invited because they had recognised her contribution to winning new business and the legal profession was like every other sector these days, enslaved to the process of sales. The good job she did in that stuffy office paid for so much of the life that she and Chicken lived that he couldn't complain about that. He could only act like a dilettante because she largely funded his lifestyle. Yes, she would be wearing her drop dead gorgeous new dress, yes she'd be meeting Thomas first for a drink and yes she would be sitting next to him through dinner, but it was all for the cause. It was oiling the wheels. It was business. Actually Chicken should be thanking her for giving up her Saturday night to stay in the good books of the firm. When she got around to telling him long after the event, who knew, perhaps he would.

Danny didn't wake on Saturday morning because he hadn't really been asleep. Dread of the coming day had kept him awake most of the night, in the same way that visits to the dentist had tormented him as a child. The night before an appointment had been a six monthly torture until he was old enough to do the brave, grown up, adult thing and stop going.
He lay in the guest bedroom, decorated as it was in a neutral and welcoming cream and listening as the house came to life around him. His sister Jane and her kids were causing the kind of friendly noise that usually comforted him, wrapping him in a cocoon of family spirit. But today was the day he would face his comedy club shame and pour salt on his still fresh wound and so the usually happy sounds felt more like a buzzing irritation. It was not right that he felt this bad, he knew it but it was out of his control. Still, there was a growing feeling inside him that perhaps there was a revenge

to exacted, some way to make it all feel better. He wouldn't be on the receiving end tonight unless someone thrust him onto the stage. That image sent a shudder through his bones.
'Do you want a cup of tea Dan?' came his sister's voice through the door.
'Ok,' he shouted back and seconds later it opened.
'Thought you might,' she beamed as she carefully placed a mug next to him. 'Bad news though.'
His heart leapt at the thought that perhaps the gig had been cancelled, or that one of the children had suffered an accident and maybe they'd all have to stay home tonight.
'What?'
'Don't look so shocked Dan, it's only raining.'
'Oh, damn.' he couldn't hide the disappointment in his voice, but Jane mistook its cause.
'Don't worry, it's just a few spots.'

Davis opened his curtains at the sounds of rain. He squinted like a fisherman judging the life threatening elements. Rain could be good and it could be bad. Not as bad as international football on terrestrial TV mind you. A big England match could kill a comedy night. The night after a big England win was fine especially if you had a comedian who knew how to milk it. Rain on the other hand could be good if it stopped punters from doing something outside and drove them in for entertainment. That's why summer was close down for Davis. Apart from Edinburgh people didn't want to sit inside listening to bitter comedy when the sun was out and they could sit at some riverside pub. And of course in the summer it was light all night. Comedy was best in the dark. However, rain could be bad if it was so torrential that everyone stayed home with their cheap supermarket larger. He eyed the weather. At the moment it was good rain, a drizzle, something you might want to be cheered up from. He checked his phone. If any comedians were going to cancel they would do it later than this but still he wanted to see if he'd had any texts. Nothing. So far so good. Good rain and no cancellations. Nothing from the management of the Grand Hotel either, and no news was good news.

The Mitsy began to splutter as rain seeped into the plugs, or some other technical area that Chicken couldn't name. Morgan didn't even seem to notice that they were now lurching alarmingly towards Scarborough.
'I hope we get there,' Chicken laughed nervously.
'We've got all day, worst case scenario we dump the car and get a bus.'
'I'm not dumping the car. Laura would kill me.'
'Ok, I dump you and the car.'
'We'll get there.'

They eventually limped into Scarborough and parked near the seafront. Chicken was in no mood for games and he was tiring of Morgan's mysterious ways.
'Ok, can we cut the crap today? Can you just tell me where the B&B is and we can go there now?'
'York.'
'We're in Scarborough and the B&B is in York, what, 45 miles away?'
'It's not a B&B. Tonight we're staying with a mate of mine, he's a writer and he lives in York and our last gig is in York, unless the TV idiots are here tonight, in which case this is our last gig.'
'So after tonight's gig we drive to York?'
'Yes, so stay sober, you have an important passenger.'
Chicken looked wearily at his watch. 'Right. We've got about nine hours. So, you're the seasoned professional. You're the rock 'n' roll comedian. What should we do?'
'Rides. Rides, arcades and then pub.'
'What about breakfast?'
'We're at the seaside. We have a responsibility to have hot donuts for breakfast my friend.'

They walked out into the drizzle of Scarborough, a strange and unknown landscape and Chicken had never felt more like an alien, and not an illegal immigrant either, a genuine Martian. There was something that felt very strange about them being there in the middle of the day and not on holiday. Morgan could see that Chicken needed some comfort, but casual cruelty was more his style.
'The guy we're doing this gig for is a bloke called Davis,' he offered. 'Total wanker. I used to see him on the London circuit, around Hackney and that, years ago but he couldn't cut it, so he came up here to run some clubs.'
'Right.'
'He's good at publicity though, so it's likely to be quite full tonight.'
'Right.' The last thing that Chicken wanted to do at that moment was contemplate comedy.
'You should make more of that bit you do about Wayne Rooney. I like that stuff, it just needs expanding a little. It's got some mileage.'
It was the first time that Morgan had ever passed comment on Chicken's act and it seemed to be positive. Chicken was secretly pleased despite himself.
'You think?'
'Yeah. I mean no one is going to laugh, but as long as I like it that's all that matters.'
The concrete sweep of the sea wall led them round and they could see that the rides were all shut for the season. It was a blessing for Chicken because he couldn't stand anything that spun him around and made him dizzy. He didn't like being lifted up high by machines either. In fact, as a kid Chicken was the type who stood holding his mates coats at the fair. It wasn't how he'd got the nickname Chicken, but it fitted. Morgan stopped walking.
'See those railings?' he was pointing down at a part of the sea wall that was lower than the rest of it, and had rusty railings to stop walkers from falling into the sea. 'Last time I was here, about two years ago, a man and his wife got

swept off there by a huge wave. They were messing about, running up to the railings, daring the sea to soak them and then rushing back. But the sea called their bluff and a really big wave came over and carried them both in. Someone jumped in to try to save them, all three drowned.'

Chicken looked to see if he was being wound up. Morgan saw his disbelief. 'It's true. I did a gig here about a week after it had happened. I'd seen it on the news, so to break the ice I made some bad joke about it as soon as I went on. I can't even remember it, something about how stupid they'd been, village idiots, something like that I think. At the end of the gig a bloke comes up to me and says that he's a distant cousin of one of the people who got washed away.'

'Oops. Was he angry?'

'No. Actually he thanked me. He said it had helped him to come to terms with it. That laughter was a good therapy.'

'He didn't!'

'Honestly, he did.'

'Wow.'

'I know. What a stupid twat. Come on let's put some money in the machines.'

Thomas Dalfin, corporate solicitor and now £750,000 per annum equity partner had learned a very hard lesson during his married life and the subsequent messy and expensive divorce. The lesson was that honesty was the most important element in any relationship. It's exactly what everyone said, but now he believed it. He had vowed that should he ever start another relationship he would insist on honesty from the start. Cover-ups and lies only led to heartache, of that he was sure. What he wasn't sure about was Laura, she was bright, funny and very attractive but she was married. True, she didn't talk much about her husband but he was probably some very rich, good looking and powerful business type. Laura had certainly brought some glamour to the staid old world of Steel and Caskett and her skills had helped to bring in some new work too. It had been quite a step for the firm to make the move into actively marketing their services and some of the senior partners still felt very uneasy about it. But they were old and didn't understand that competition these days was fierce and although they were never going to get into ambulance chasing they had certainly seen the benefits of employing someone whose job it was to, well, how could you put it? Sell. Nothing too flashy, more about brand recognition and underlining the traditional values. Dignity had been preserved and business had been won against competition from other larger firms, and that was one of the reasons that tonight's dinner had been arranged. It was a celebration, a recognition and an acceptance.

Her professional competence aside, the interesting point was that Laura certainly seemed to be interested in him and he felt flattered and emboldened by her attention. It was a slight dilemma but really it was for her to work out if there were any issues with her husband, after all, people got divorced every day. They had to, it was a revenue stream for the bread and butter legal market. Still, the fact remained that truth was key. From the start, and perhaps this was a starting point?

Chicken had an uneasy feeling that he was in the wrong place at the wrong time. There were so many 'right' things he should be doing in 'right' places, and for one thing his lack of activity on his freelance design work would surely bite him hard next month. No income plus unusual outgoings was a recipe for hard times and he knew it. When he got back he'd have to grovel and try to rebuild his relationship with Duncan at the design studio after letting him down badly on that caravan advert job. Duncan had been a steady, reliable source of work for a few years now and Chicken realised that he'd been taking it for granted. Madness really to let such easy money slip through his fingers.

He put another 10 pence in the slot and watched it bounce down through the pins before coming to rest on the moving upper shelf. It fitted nicely into a gap without dislodging anything onto the second, lower shelf, which therefore didn't result in any sort of payout. He'd put in 80 pence so far and he was counting every penny. Next to him Morgan's machine showered him with silver, a noisy avalanche that must have come to at least a pound or maybe more. Morgan moved to the automated horse racing machine behind them and bet on red. They watched the tiny plastic thoroughbreds go through their paces. The long odds green was out in front for most of the race but Chicken just nodded when the red jacketed jockey came in first.

The Vegas Arcade was pretty empty but the various electronic noises and flashing lights tried hard to give the impression of a hive of wild activity. On many of the machines small plastic bowls lay waiting to be filled with change and the booth where all the money ultimately ended up housed a bored teenager. Like a lot of deserted fun palaces, an air of sadness hung in the gloom.

Chicken left Morgan in the arcade and wandered off to find a phone. His mobile was out of battery and he had forgotten to bring his charger. Morgan's phone was out of credit and Chicken knew that if he was to use it he would have to be the one to top it up. It was difficult to find a public phone but he had a real need to speak to Laura. Eventually he found a payphone in the lobby of a hotel and rang home but his heart sank a little when he heard his own recorded voice. He waited for the beep, just as he'd instructed himself to do. 'Um, hi, it's me. Hope you're ok. My phone's dead and I haven't got a charger. It's going really well, the tour. No, it really is. Anyway, I'll be back very late Sunday night. I'll try to call later maybe after tonight's gig. You must be out at the shops or something. In the shower maybe? Whatever, hope you're ok. Love you. Bye.' The call had left him unsatisfied and there was something about his cocky tone on the answer message that had annoyed him. Who did he think he was?

Chicken found Morgan where he'd left him and they walked out to survey the crumbling architectural beauty of Scarborough. As they walked Morgan nudged Chicken's arm at the approach of a fat, tattooed family tucking into their early morning cones of chips.

The tide was out so they walked down onto the large open beach and felt the whip of the north eastern winds. There were people with dogs, kids trying to play cricket and families huddled inside the odd beach tent or two. They strolled all the way along to the North Bay and could see the brightly coloured pastel beach huts up beyond the sea wall. There were some surfers out, bobbing around in their black wetsuits, stamping down on brightly coloured boards perched momentarily on grey waves under grey skies.

'This is what it's all about,' said Morgan smiling broadly.

'What do you mean? All what's about?'

'Turning up in some strange town, pissing around all day like kids bunking off school and then doing a gig. What could be better?'

'Getting paid?

'You're on the learning curve buddy, this is your college course. You can't learn comedy in your bedroom, you have to get in front of a live audience. I'm doing you a favour here.'

'Thanks.'

'Besides, what else would you be doing with your life anyway?'

'Getting paid.'

'Really? Oh sorry, I thought you said getting laid, but then I remembered that you're married.' Chicken laughed despite himself. Morgan pressed on. 'Come on, the pubs are open let's find somewhere to have a drink.'

'I can't drink before a show. It makes me confused and I forget my jokes.'

'Don't be so anal, it's the middle of the day, you've got plenty of time to sober up before the gig.'

Laura stepped from the shower room swathed in fluffy towels and then seeing the blinking red light on the phone listened to the message from Chicken. So, his phone was dead which meant that she couldn't reach him. She shrugged, if he hadn't had the sense to make sure he packed his charger it wasn't her fault. He was off, doing exactly what he wanted to do, enjoying himself on some kind of boys jolly. Well it was his choice, he had chosen, without her consultation to take off and leave her alone. She crossed to the bedroom and flopped on the bed with a satisfied sigh. No one to fight over the bathroom with, no one to cook breakfast for, plenty of room and plenty of time to get ready for tonight, it was almost like being single again.

Chicken wasn't used to having a whole day to think about a gig and it was an odd situation to be in. On a normal day he'd be working at his computer, lost in the time absorbing world of graphic design for the day. But now, with such a lot of time to fill the pre-gig nerves that were always mixed with a genuine but painful excitement started to kick in early. They had found a pub eager for their trade and settled comfortably. There was the obligatory flashing fruit machine cycling through its enticing visual display and a flat screen TV switched to Sky on the wall. It wasn't crowded and the two comedians were able to spread out on an upholstered corner seat with newspapers on their table. The first couple of lunchtime pints slipped down easily, somewhat damping down Chicken's nerves and he started to feel that he could quite easily sit there all day. Maybe forever.
Morgan was in a more sombre mood than usual.
'I'm starting to think that I'm not going to see any big-shot TV execs at these gigs. I think it's a lie and that I've been jerked around by that arsehole of an agent of mine.'
'Why would he do that?'
'Because he's a sadistic bastard.'
'At least you have an agent. At least you don't have to chase gigs all the time.'

'I still chase, believe me.'
'But it's easy for you Morgan, you've got the name and people know who you are so you're set up now. That's you for life.' Morgan shook his head solemnly.
'It doesn't work like that. You never know. I did a benefit gig recently, actually I couldn't do it because I was busy, but it was for a home that looks after these retired performers. Amazing. Guys who have nothing left, no money, no family but you'd be staggered by how many of them were really big in their day. Faces you'd see on TV the whole time. But styles change, audiences change, they get younger and nothing stands still and the public is fickle. If you're out of fashion, you're out of fashion.'
'I guess.'
'Look at Frankie Howerd. He was at the very top, went out of fashion, didn't work for absolutely years. Not until post ironic uni students discovered that he knew how to tell a joke.'
Morgan picked up his beer and stared hard at Chicken.
'Maybe we should just forget Scarborough and York and just go home now?'
'But you're booked.'
'Fuck 'em. It's only Davis, who cares?'
'We're not jacking it in now Morgan, we're here for Christ's sake, we've done the driving, or I have, and you need to get paid because if nothing else you owe me money. You owe me petrol and you owe me for the accommodation.'
Morgan grinned through the last of his pint and then stood up to get another.
'Don't worry mate I'm only winding you up. I'm a professional. It's show business and the show WILL go on.'
He patted Chicken on the shoulder. 'Can you lend me a tenner for drinks?

Davis got to the Grand Hotel at 6pm a full two hours before the show was due to start in order to set everything up. The public address system and microphones had to be checked, especially tonight as one of the acts was a comedy guitarist.

The semi-musical acts, with their funny songs always went down well, Davis couldn't imagine why, he hated them, and most other comedians considered it 'cheating', but the punters loved them – so Davis put them on.

He ran the comedy club in the basement function area that had its own bar and small stage. It was perfect really if not a little cramped. The venue was important, it helped and that's why Davis really didn't want to lose it. The maximum safe head-count in the room was 150, but to be honest it was rare to get that many.

He had to make sure that the poster upstairs in the main bar of the hotel clearly led the people down to the comedy and he needed to put a flyer on every table with details of the next week's gig.

For him, the fun part of the evening would be his own compering. He was the hilarious comedy glue that would stick the whole show together. He would kick the thing off, do some jokes and welcome everyone, he would find out who they had in tonight and take the piss out of one or two. There would be a hard-core of regulars who knew him and he'd try to build some noisy enthusiasm for all the acts. He would also be running a competition based on the audience providing a funny caption to a photo that was on every table.

As Davis went around distributing a photocopy of an elephant that had walked into a supermarket, for the competition, he realised that there was someone behind him. It was Ray, the new manager of the Hotel and he was smiling his sickly smile.

'Hi, putting out the old flyers?' he picked up the photo. 'Caption competition? Funny old picture isn't it?'

Davis nodded and carried on putting them out.

'That's the idea Ray, funny picture, funny caption and some lucky member of the crowd gets to win a mars bar.'

'So, have we got some good comedians tonight?'

Davis did not like the 'we'. 'I always book good comedians Ray, it comes from my 15 years in the business. I know them all, personally. I know who's going to do well and who

to avoid. Of course Scarborough is a bit out of the way for a lot of the London guys, but I put in the call and they generally respond.'
'Right. Should be a good old night then. A grand old night even.' He laughed. 'Grand. Oh, I should have been a comedian.'
Davis straightened up and looked him straight in the eye. 'You know what Ray, if you want to try an open spot I'd put you on. If you'd fancy it?' Davis was itching to get the pompous arse out there in front of a live audience and watch him squirm. He'd seen so often how that one small step from the wings to centre stage could destroy an ego.'
'No, it's ok, my performing days are over. Did a bit of am-dram a few years back but that was it for me.'
'You sure Ray? You'd enjoy it.'
'No, thanks, I'm just interested in keeping the customers happy these days.'
'Me too Ray, that's why I take such a lot of care over booking acts.'
'It's a great venue for comedy though isn't it? This basement really works.'
'It's ok.'
'And the venue is soooo important isn't it?'
'Comedians. That's what's important Ray. Comedians. And access to drink. The rest is just wrapping paper.'

'Come on Danny, we're going to be late. We don't want to miss the first act,' Jane shouted up the stairs.
'I'm in the toilet, I'll be out in a minute.' Danny had a choice and now was the last minute to make it, he could fake an illness, and to be honest it wouldn't be too difficult with the way his stomach felt, or he could brave it out. He really didn't want to be brave but he could see the advantage of facing his shame head on, especially up here in Scarborough as no one would know about his previous disaster. There were no well-meaning workmates to make excruciating comments like, 'remember the time you tried

that?' He could sit quietly, have plenty to drink and then it would all be over. It was time to face his demons and face the future. He stood up, pulled up his trousers and looked into the pan. 'My future.' he mumbled.

Laura wanted to be at the bar for 7:30, they weren't due at the meal until 8:30 so it would give her an hour to chat with Thomas away from the scrutiny of the people from work. She could act cool and reserved but make sure that he noticed how fantastic she looked. She got out of the taxi in front of the bar and could see Thomas at a table near the window. That was good, it meant that she wouldn't have to do that lonely sit waiting for him to turn up, but then Thomas would never have left her sitting there, that much she knew. As she swung the door open she had to remind herself that it wasn't a date. Not a real date anyway. For some weird reason for a tiny second she thought of her first date with Chicken. The pub in Hackney arranged for a mutual friend's birthday and then the Indian restaurant that they had gone to afterwards. Nothing spectacular, no sudden jolt of passion, but a lot of fun. It was a memory that always made her smile, so she was smiling pleasantly as she joined Thomas, who assuming that she was happy to see him smiled back.
'Well, if it's not too forward of me to say so Laura, you do look fantastic. Somehow everyone looks different outside work don't they, not that you don't look fantastic at work, I just mean it's always strange in a new environment.'
Laura nodded. He was certainly verbally gushing like he was on a date.
'Thanks, and you look as smart as ever Thomas, although you are probably wearing exactly the same as you wear to the office I imagine.'
'Well, it sort of is the office isn't it? On parade with the senior partners? They aren't really the type to let their hair down. So anyway, what will you have?'

Laura hesitated, this was one of those evenings where she absolutely couldn't afford to get drunk though the lure of wine was strong.
'White wine,' she said. 'Large.'

Chicken was not drunk, he'd exercised some self control as the day had worn on, but it hadn't been easy. The relaxed and carefree atmosphere of being in a pub during daylight hours had eroded his willpower and so had the regular trips with his money bar by Morgan. At about four o'clock Chicken had impressively marshalled his forces and moved on to soft drinks. He'd also ordered a bar meal, something breaded and perched on a mountain of chips. By six he may not have been drunk but he wasn't sharp either.
Morgan had topped his mobile phone up and was using up his new minutes on Matty his agent.
'Right, so now you actually know something Matty. So now you tell me. They are going to be in York tomorrow, but not Scarborough tonight? That's what you're telling me? The media whores won't go to the seaside, but genteel and historic York is fine. I know it's too late to cancel, and I'm not going to cancel, because I have my professional reputation to think of. Those people in Scarborough are MY audience, they've paid to see ME and that's what they are going to see. So don't worry, your commission is safe.' He cut the phone off.
'Not at tonight's gig then?' ventured Chicken.
'Nope. Maybe we should cancel and just get another beer?'
'Cancel? Why? I don't get it? I thought you liked being a comedian? Why do you always want to cancel?'
For the first time a certain honesty leaked from Morgan.
'Because I shouldn't be doing these little gigs Chicken, they're chicken shit. I'm above this now and I shouldn't be going backwards. If I allow myself to drop down to shit holes then everything I've been working for over 15 years is lost. I should be playing the big rooms now. That arse is making me jump through hoops, for his 15% of nothing.'

'Morgan, I'm not getting paid and I still want to do the gig. It'll be fun, and fuck, we're here.'
'Well, get me a drink and I'll think about it.'

They got there early which gave them a good choice of empty tables, in fact too much choice so they stood lost in a sea of chairs scanning around for the perfect landing point. Danny had been introduced to Jane's friends outside, two pleasant enough couples, but he was too stressed to listen properly and now couldn't remember any of the names. Thankfully Jane hadn't done the plotting sister thing and invited a single woman to even out the numbers.
'Oh, God, if you sit near the front the comedians pick on you,' one of the women was screeching with a definite note of glee in her voice, as if to say, 'it would be terrible BUT I'd love it.'
'Yeah, but if we're too far back we won't see much,' said Brian. One of the other men agreed with that.
'Gotta get your money's worth, I think we should sit close to the front, we won't miss anything then. I want to see the bloke off the yoghurt ad.'
'Dan's the guest, let him choose,' chipped in Jane, ever the caring sister.
They turned to Dan. He desperately wanted to be at the back away from the action, but under the spotlight of being designated the decider he also didn't want to appear to care one way or the other, so he mumbled,
'Sort of middle I suppose,' and pointed at a table.
'Right, drinks.' announced someone and moved off to the bar. They seemed like a reasonable bunch, thought Danny, fairly middle-class and all older than him, in their mid thirties, he guessed. They didn't appear to be the types to shout obscenities at the stage. He'd thought about that possibility. If one of Jane's friend's turned out to be an arsehole, would he be able to keep his mouth shut out of respect for Jane and her husband? Would he be able to ignore it and stop

himself from punching the friend if he, or she, was an ignorant heckler?
When they got back with the drinks one of the friends, the man who looked most like he was probably an accountant, said, 'I just hope there aren't any of those beginners.'
'What do you mean?' asked Jane.
'You know, sometimes they give new people a go and they are always awful.'
His partner joined in.
'Oh yes, it's painful to watch, you're just like dreading it and you just want them to stop.'
'It's like the worst acts on X factor.'
'God, yes it's totally embarrassing.'
'But it can be sort of fun seeing how bad they are.'
'Yeah, like a freak show thing.'
Danny said absolutely nothing but under the table his fists were clenching and unclenching.

As they walked towards the Grand Hotel, Chicken realised that he was much drunker than he'd felt in the dingy confines of the pub earlier and now in the fresh air he was wondering if he'd given himself enough time to sober up. At the moment his words were still flowing though and he was hoping he could get it together for his act. He started going over his opening line in his mind, over and over again to prime the pump. He recognised the faint tightening of his rectum that signalled a necessary visit to the toilet.
'So you've never told me, why did you want to be a comedian?' he asked Morgan, who seemed to be showing no signs of having any alcohol in his blood at all although he'd actually drunk twice as much as Chicken. Without hesitating Morgan launched straight into a story that he's obviously told more than once.
'When I was a kid, in the days before the internet, I got all my best education from an old, retro Playboy magazine that my dad had in the shed. I'm not just talking about learning what tits looked like or fannies for that matter, I mean what

was happening out there in America land. Where the glamour and action was. One of dirty the mags was from nineteen seventy something and it had a poll of the world's sexiest men. As voted for by Playboy Playmates, which was the only kind of vote I was interested in. At number one was Burt Reynolds, who was a big star at the time and fairly obvious as a sex symbol. Muscles, moustache, you know this was before gay had taken that look. I knew I couldn't be Burt, so I sort of skipped him. But at number two was Woody Allen.'
'Genius,' nodded Chicken.
'The Playmates all said that his sense of humour was really, sexy and that they'd all like to sleep with him, even though he looked like shit. Or as close to those words as they were allowed to say in the 70s. Anyway, I was young and easily influenced and I thought that if I could be as funny as Woody Allen I could be as sexy and popular with women. That was it. I didn't really want to be a comedian, if they'd said number two was a shoe salesman, then that's what I'd be doing now.'
'Yeah, it's a fallacy. Girls don't really like comedians. There is no such thing as a comedy groupie, at least I've never seen one.'
'I know, but it was a long time before I realised what a load of old crap it was and it was too late by then, I'd already fucked up at school.'

They arrived at the Grand Night Out comedy club, wound their way down the stairs and immediately bumped into Davis. Morgan was in some kind of angry mood and was pretty short with him.
'Hi, listen Davis, this is Chicken, he's with me. He needs to do an open spot tonight if possible.'
The man Davis, who was sporting a kind of Russell Brand rock dude image, grimaced. He hadn't even looked at Chicken yet.

'Can't really do it Morgan. We've got a pretty tight show tonight, I've got Dougie Hendrix, I'm doing some stuff myself, I've got Len Bishop in the middle, a competition then you. There's not really room for an open.'
Before Chicken could get upset, Morgan winked at him.
'OK Davis, that's cool, and as it happens you've got more room now for your own stuff because I'm off.' He stepped towards the door. 'This poor fucker has driven me all the way from London, and if he can't get an open, then I'm going straight back again.'
Losing his headliner with minutes to go was not an option that Davis was ever going to seriously consider, and one look at Morgan's face told him that he meant what he said. 'I didn't say he couldn't do one. Did I say that? Of course not. It's cool.' He turned to Chicken. 'Can you keep it to ten?'
'Sure. And thanks.'
'No problem.' As he moved away Chicken was sure he heard Davis mutter, 'Fucking comedians' under his breath.

When Dougie Hendrix came out into the light Danny immediately recognised him as the guitar comedian who had been the act on before him at his comedy nightmare. He shrank in his seat, certain that he would be seen and remembered, perhaps even become the butt of Dougie's act. He could almost hear it, 'Oh, look over here we have a real loser in tonight.'
What Danny didn't know was that if he had climbed up on stage, bitten Hendrix on the hand and asked if he remembered a poor sod who'd followed him on stage, and then died on his arse, Dougie's answer would certainly have been no. He might have asked why he'd been bitten on the hand but he didn't even remember the gig in question or anything that had happened at it. And right now, he was blinded by his own brilliance. Dougie Hendrix was loud, his songs were snatches of well known riffs with mutilated lyrics finishing on punch lines and it generally went over very well. The recognition factor of hearing the first few bars of a song

that everybody knows somehow worked in his favour, and Doug was good at working it.
Danny sat, watched, listened and carefully analysed. It wasn't funny but everyone was laughing. As he took in the enjoyment of everyone around him his overriding emotion was no longer fear or shame it was jealousy, pure burning envy heated by a streak of anger.

Eventually Dougie finished on an ear-blasting classic and was wildly applauded as he left the stage to be replaced by Davis. Jane patted Dan's arm and grinned.
'He was good wasn't he?'
'He was alright. Bit old fashioned maybe. Bit clichéd.'
'I loved it,' said one of the accountants.
'So funny.'
'That was ace.'
Dan stood.
'I'll get the drinks.'

'Shall we go?'
She really didn't want to leave this utterly charming place. It was so nice in the bar, so bright, vibrant and exciting, so full of the movers and shakers of London. Laura felt for the first time in her life that she was right at the heart of something important. More than that she was actually taking part in the high-life rather than playing the interested spectator.
Chicken's cynical voice wasn't chiming in, picking faults and trying to stoke a working class resentment. Without him there was no one constantly searching for 'the joke'.
The conversation with Thomas had been work based but so stimulating that the thought of moving on now was slightly disappointing but it was a short distance to the restaurant and the dinner wasn't just a dinner, it was a career enhancing social event. It was part of a series of fortunate events that had started at the time that Thomas had rescued her bag on the train. All good signs. She hauled herself out of the red leather armchair.

'Let's get to my dinner,' she said.
'By the way,' asked Thomas as they stepped out into the busy night, 'I hope you've told your husband all about this. I wouldn't want to be accosted by an angry husband in the street,' he laughed to show this was an absurd idea. 'I'm big on honesty,' he added.
'Me too,' said Laura. 'He knows all about it but he's away on business at the moment, so he couldn't possibly come.'
'Somewhere exotic I bet?'
'Yes, Scarborough.' It was out of her mouth before she could stop herself. Thomas didn't break stride probably thinking that she'd made a joke.
'There's the restaurant,' he said pointing across the road and Laura looked at a slick vision of light and glass that sent a tickle through her insides. It was the kind of place that said, ordinary people don't come here, only the elite.
'Wow.'
'Never been?'
'No.'
'Well I can tell you, the food's as great as you've heard. But you'd expect that from Jago Steller's flagship restaurant wouldn't you?'
'Oh, right, of course. Chicken's got one of his books,' Thomas frowned, not recognising the name that she had never uttered. How do you explain a name like that?
'Pardon?'
'I said, I've seen chicken recipes in his books. So you've been before?'
'Oh, once or twice,' he answered smiling.

Danny's beer fuelled anger was mounting and it started to spill a little when Len Bishop took to the stage. Len was a laid back comedian who lulled rather than shook his audience, at one point during some quiet seconds while he seemed to be gathering his thoughts Danny felt, 'Get on with it.' On the tip of his tongue. When Len turned to look at him Danny realised that it hadn't stayed on his tongue or in his

mouth. He really had said it out loud. Slowly Len lowered his glasses and over the top of them said,
'Easy tiger.' It got an enormous laugh and Danny's pulse began to race as his breath quickened. The comedian shrugged. Which drove the audience wild. 'There's more where that came from.' he added like an old man telling off a child, which was exactly what the crowd wanted to hear. Everyone at Danny's table was looking a little shocked. One of the women leaned over to him.
'Oh, Danny, that's what they do. If you shout out they take the piss out of you.'
'No shit,' said Danny which even caused Jane to glower at him.

Sometimes, thought Laura, all the planets are in alignment, all the stars are pulling together, all the shit is cleared away and things go right for you. This was such a night. The Partners, and their very welcoming partners had all treated Laura like a guest of honour. It was wonderful and only very slightly patronising. And there was no Chicken to have to make excuses for or to mess it up. Instead there was Thomas, smiling and attentive and appearing to enjoy the evening as much as she was. Before anyone could ask she explained very quickly that her husband was away on business and then directed the attention onto other matters, like the dazzling beauty of the napkin rings and the interestingly shaped cutlery.

Laura had married Chicken back in the days when money didn't matter, when it was all in front of them and riches would surely come along at some point so there was nothing to worry about, was there? They both had jobs, albeit low paid starting point positions, Chicken in a design studio and her in the marketing department of a software company. They had been in love, what more was there to say? They got married when many of their ex-college friends were simply co-habiting but they ignored that trend, not for any religious reasons either. Having met him through a mutual friend Laura had instantly liked Chicken who had been different from her business studies usuals. He was interesting, creative, artistic and fun. And fairly good looking too, in a face full of character kind of way. However, she now often thought that many of the traits that he had weren't the kinds of traits that she would list on an internet dating site as her ideals for a match these days. For instance, he found it hard to take anything seriously, even serious things that really needed to be taken seriously. It was one of those attributes that had gone from charming to irritating over the years. She had often wondered if that was why he had been prepared to get married without the usual male commitment issues and the long strung out engagement. He hadn't taken it seriously.

He had mentioned to her early on in their relationship (or as he referred to it at the time as more of a relation-boat than a full on relation-ship, and she found *that* funny!) that he liked comedy and that he had done some open mic spots at the student's union when he was at art college. She hadn't paid any attention at the time. A few years later, when he told her casually that he was going out one Friday night to try out at a local comedy club she still didn't pay much attention. The one night developed into a couple a month and after about a year she was paying attention and he was calling himself a comedian.

Chicken was aware that the sneaky ability of alcohol to make you think that you're very funny when you are not could be disastrous for a would-be comedian. Of greater concern though was the confusing, befuddling and memory suppressing effects of having a drink, even if that drink was several hours before as it had now been. Chicken's biggest fear was that he would forget everything in his act and stand gaping like a fish. A comedy salmon flapping around on the stage. At a boozy dinner party when he lost his thread it was never a problem, he could sit silently letting Laura take the

strain until the genius idea came back but under the glare of audience expectation every second felt like a painful lifetime. Chicken had been watching when the heckler had shouted out to Len and he had nodded appreciatively when Len had so easily dealt with him. Now the young guy had shut up, so hopefully he would stay shut up. Morgan who was standing next to him at the back was less sanguine.
'That little git. He better not start that shit with me. I'm not in the mood.'
Davis was chatting away on stage and then issued a rallying cry and suddenly it was time.

At the mic Chicken started slowly but even on his tried and tested opening he stumbled a little over his words. The crowd, buoyed up by the fun they'd been having up until that point were patient until after hearing three gags they still hadn't heard anything that they thought was funny. The coughing and shuffling started. It was possibly due to the subtle grip of alcohol, or perhaps the fear of what it might be doing but Chicken's timing was all wrong and he knew it. He was distracted. Comedy was all about the image that you projected on stage and tonight Chicken's image was of someone who didn't know what he was doing. He was just not 'hitting' the punch lines.
From the dark, a voice, the voice, shouted,
'You are shit.'
Chicken responded with 'easy tiger,' it was meant ironically, as an echo of Len, but it just sounded like he was lost and copying the previous comedian. The voice got louder and more aggressive, hissing with hate. 'You are such a hopeless wanker. Think of a funny joke. Say something funny, what have you come here for? Why are you up there? Think of a funny joke.' The rest of the audience sat in embarrassed silence.
This was exactly where he should take control but Chicken couldn't think of anything clever to say so he carried on with his act as if the guy wasn't there. It wasn't great. At one point

the heckler began to bark like a dog, over and over again. Chicken ignored it. What could he say to a dog? Actually there was plenty to say but he just couldn't think of it at that moment. He blanked out everything around him and soldiered on to the end. It was what a professional would do. He smiled.

'Thank you, you've been great,' and then walked off.

At the table Jane, Brian and their friends were fussing with coats getting ready to leave, but up on stage Morgan had shoved his way past Davis and come on without waiting to be introduced.

'Hello. Nice to see you all here in sunny Scarborough, and it's particularly nice to meet you.' He pointed at Danny. 'Because tonight is dedicated to you. Someone just committed the crime of trying to make you laugh, when what they should have committed was the other crime. Murder.'

There was an enormous wave of agreement and thunderous applause from everyone who had been embarrassed or simply tired of the pointless heckling. It wasn't what they'd paid to hear, but now they did get their money's worth. Morgan ditched his usual act and made Danny his act. It was savage. The frustration of the whole pointless tour poured out into the air as Morgan ridiculed and ripped. He had a wealth of put downs and insults and his bald head bobbed like a boxer as he relentlessly pushed on. When the heckler tried to respond he was drowned out and buried, when he barked he was lost in the sound of laughing directed at him. It wasn't Morgan's usual style, and for Chicken watching from the sidelines who had already seen his act many times it had an edge of aggression and bitterness that he hadn't seen before. Every single joke and reference was expertly woven around to include the heckler. Listening, Chicken was in total admiration. Morgan certainly had the gift and maybe it was the confidence of knowing that he could always go to this that made everything else he did so strong.

Danny couldn't believe it. He had felt so strong for a while, making the chicken squirm like he had squirmed. He'd come out with some funny bits too, the barking had seemed cool. The guy was a dog of a comedian so he had barked, surely they could see that? But then this. A stream that took him straight back to the stage of his death. They were laughing at him, with undisguised malice. With hatred even. He'd been the victim when he'd been on stage and now he was the target off it.
Jane and Brian, and all of their friends were sitting with fixed smiles as if they were getting the joke and enjoying it but Danny could see that all they wanted was for it to end. None of them dared stand up to leave. To stand would show that they had been completely beaten. Worse it would draw even more attention to them and supply more ammunition so they sat and smiled.
The unexpected thing for Danny was that he suddenly felt very sorry for the guy he'd heckled. It was true, he just been trying to make them laugh.

At the bar Davis was laughing and nodding at it all. Ray tapped him on the shoulder.
'I think you should stop it.'
'What?'
'Get up there as compere and stop him. He's too offensive. He's foul mouthed. He called him a cunt and I don't want any trouble in here.'
Davis was incredulous.
'Don't you get it? They'll be talking about this for months. They are loving it.' He swept his hand across the room to indicate the crowd. 'They are loving it. This is what live comedy is about. This is why they aren't at home watching the TV. This is what the Grand Night Out needs.'
'I don't think so. I think maybe it might be time for this club to take a new more upmarket direction.'
'That twat came in here to ruin the show and Morgan has rescued the night. This is comedy gold.'

'Listen, we've got plans for this place and the other clubs in our chain and I think there should be certain standards.'
'Plans? What plans.'
Before Ray could answer their attention was drawn to the stage. Ray need not have worried about getting him off because at that moment Morgan came to the end of his stint and with a wave exited the stage. The Heckler's table stood as one and left, followed by resounding cheers from the crowd. In the noise Davis bounded on stage and took the mic.
'Hope you've had a great night. That was special and that's the kind of excellent live comedy that I bring you at this club, so let's hear it again for Morgan.' There was a loud cheer. 'But before you go let me just say that there might be some changes happening soon. The management don't like the fun you've been having and so the club might be closing.' There was general end of evening confusion going on and this wasn't helping. 'The club may be moving venue so keep your eyes on the website. If you want to keep seeing comedy as good as this, stick with me, I'll see you right.'

Morgan and Chicken hung around long enough to get Morgan's money from Davis, who was still hyped up and muttering away about betrayal and back-stabbing. He wanted to discuss it with Morgan but Morgan wasn't interested and Chicken certainly wasn't. Once they had the cash they immediately headed out with barely a backward glance.
'Listen, I'll email you about where the new club will be,' shouted Davis after them. 'Always got a gig for you Morgan. And nice seeing you ...' he tailed off, unable to remember Chicken's name.
'Sure,' said Morgan stuffing the notes in his pocket. As they made their way through the last of the audience Chicken got a few pitying smiles and pats on the back from the stragglers, and Morgan got huge number of loud back slaps. They said nothing until they were in the car.

'It was my own fault,' said Chicken. 'I was crap tonight. Crap. They see a weakness and they go for it.'
'Forget it. He was a twat,' answered Morgan, 'and the real lesson from tonight, if you're going to make it in this game, is that one's over, on to the next.'
Fortunately it hadn't been raining and during its rest the Mitsubishi had dried out nicely so the car started easily.
'You were amazing Morgan, brilliant.'
'Yeah, thanks, but not TV friendly, so it's just as well that the pampered execs are waiting in York.'
'It's pretty late now, are we going to your mate's? Will he still be up at this time?'
'Don't worry, he's a writer, he never sleeps.'
Chicken pretended that he had done as Morgan suggested and put the night behind him, but both men in the car knew that he hadn't.
'Do you know who used to drive me between gigs?' asked Morgan to break the painful silence. 'Have you seen Harry Steadford on the box? Smartarse Challenge and the rest of those shows?'
'Him?'
'Yup. We started at the same time, went to the same gigs followed each other on. He had a good agent and got a couple of breaks, and I'm still waiting for mine. He's in a TV studio as we speak and I'm still travelling the North. So when that tit piped up tonight I had some strong feelings of frustration to vent.'
'He caught both barrels.'
He was too stupid or too drunk to know how honoured he was.'

Jane sat on the edge of her brother's bed, in the pleasantly decorated guest room as he lay staring at the pleasantly painted ceiling. They had driven home in silence and their friends had made their own ways home.
'I'm sorry, if I embarrassed your friends tonight.'

'Don't worry about them they're grownups, I'm worried about you. That wasn't you tonight Danny, what on earth is the matter?'

'It's so stupid Jane, I'd be ashamed to tell you. I had something that I needed to get out of my system.' And then of course he told her all of it. She listened calmly.

'And that's it? You had a little go on stage and that turned you into a moron?'

'I know. I told you it was stupid.'

'Is it your job? Is it drugs? Is it a relationship?'

'No, it really was that one open spot. But I guess you're right, there must be more to it than that. It opened something up in me. Why can't I just shrug it off like any normal person would? I feel like I lost all my self-respect, my dreams, everything. I'm not the person I thought I was.'

'You had ONE go Dan. Maybe that's just the start, Maybe you need to get back on the horse. Try again?'

'No. No. No. I couldn't do it again. I couldn't face that again. I'm too thin skinned. I can see that now.'

'But do you think any of these comedians were good when they first started? They just stuck at it. You've always made me laugh.' Jane got up. 'You might want to apologise to Brian though, he got the tickets.'

'I will.'

'All I can say is if this open spot upset you so much then it must have really meant something to you and it's got to be worth another shot.' She left and closed the door behind her.

'No, it doesn't. What I need is to forget about it now. It's over. Get back to life.'

He turned on the TV which was standing on top of the chest of drawers. The sound of laughter preceded the picture which was Harry Steadford's 'cheeky' face, the comedian of the moment who seemed to be on every channel every minute of the day and night. Danny clicked the TV straight off without trying to find a Steadford free programme.

'This isn't going to be easy,' he murmured to himself.

The meal was delicious. After a whisper of a starter, that cheekily featured a blue cheese smear on a daring lattice of grilled seaweed, Laura had chosen salmon for her main course. It was presented in a preposterously elaborate contrivance that left the fish looking like a swan and included small round things in the centre of the plate that could have been gooseberries, or perhaps balls of mashed sardine. She wasn't sure, and she wasn't going to ask.

There were five senior partners at the table along with their beautifully manicured wives. Surprisingly to Laura the conversation did not centre around work, in fact there seemed to be some sort of rule in operation that prevented the office being mentioned. Instead the talk was about parties, successful children, second homes and wonderful restaurants. These people are cultured, thought Laura, and glancing at Thomas she saw how well he fitted in. He was by far the youngest man at the meal, and certainly the most handsome. She thought of Chicken right now on a stage in a northern seaside town, saying dirty words to dirty people. She winced as she imagined one of the old partners leaning over to him were he here and asking which firm he worked for. Chicken would have to make a joke of it. The last time he was asked a question like that he'd answered, me, I'm with Back, Crack and Sack. She sniggered quietly. Actually it was quite funny when she thought about it now. Instinctively she found herself hoping that he was alright, but then she pushed it to one side with the thought that he was where he had chosen to be tonight. He could have been here with her, at this incredible meal. If she'd told him about it.

Thomas was sitting on Laura's right and to her left was Mr Chase, who was the oldest and most senior partner of them all. He had a reputation as a ruthless operator especially when it came to protecting the firm but Laura had never found him to be anything other than friendly and professional in her dealings with him. Tonight he was positively charming. He was attentive in a fatherly way, going out of his way to ensure that she didn't feel out of place.

The courses appeared and disappeared and the wine flowed easily but not in an alkie on a bench kind of way, more like an ancient and respectable stream on a country estate. She struggled somewhat with the dessert which continuing a theme was some sort of fish ice-cream. However, no sooner had it arrived than a buzz went through the room. Jago Steller, the owner and celebrity chef himself was amongst them, with his Latin good looks and his pristine white chef's coat. Laura recognised him from the TV and was as star-struck as everyone else. He moved through the tables having a word here and there, dispensing jollity all around before he stopped at theirs.
'Hello, lovely lady,' he said to Laura. 'I hope you enjoyed your meal?'
It was very strange to be addressed by a face that usually beamed at her from the cover of a book that Chicken liked to swear 'You're only a fucking cook' at.
'Oh, it was wonderful. Thank you. So, fishy.'
Jago turned to Thomas. 'You're a lucky guy,' he winked at him.
'Thanks,' said Thomas. And then Jago did something quite unexpected and extraordinary, he roared with laughter and grabbed Thomas lifting him out of his seat in a hug.
'Why didn't you tell me you were coming in Tommy?'
'I didn't know you'd be here. Anyway, it's a work thing.' Jago took in the rest of the table.
'Well I'm very sorry ladies and gentlemen for interrupting but Tommy and I go way back.' There was a chorus of 'Oh, it's fine, don't worry, anytime.' He pointed at Thomas, 'And let me tell you. That boy can cook. Call me,' he said frowning accusingly at Thomas as he rolled off to the next table.
'You didn't tell me you knew him,' said Laura. Thomas had a confused expression on his face,
'Knew who?' Laura laughed. A lot.

When they left the restaurant and said goodbye to the others, some of whom had actual cars with drivers, it was very natural that they shared a taxi, because it could drop Thomas off on the way to Laura's. When they reached his flat it was then quite logical and sensible that she should stop in for a night-cap, a coffee to sober up a bit and get a taxi the rest of the way later.

It was a lovely flat, beautifully decorated and tastefully furnished. There was wood, there was leather and there were shiny things that were probably solid silver. It absolutely reeked of money and interior designers. And this was only the place he used during the week. She couldn't imagine how the country house must be, especially with its glorious new kitchen extension. She sank into the plush kitchen sofa with a mug of freshly brewed java.
'That was great, wasn't it?' he asked as he sat next to her. 'The whole evening I mean? Everyone was very impressed with you Laura. I think you'll have done your prospects a lot of good tonight.'
'Really? Are you sure? I didn't have that much to contribute.' Of course she was fishing a little, she knew that she'd been impressive in an understated sort of way.
'Ah but you did it with style, and if nothing else Steel and Caskett is about style. On a social level you were completely acceptable and it goes a long way at a firm like this.'
Acceptable, thought Laura, quite a compliment.
It was very quiet, even with the classical music playing softly in the background. He turned to study her and a serious look crossed his face.
'It's very late and it's time to be honest Laura.' She felt her breath stick in her throat.
'Is it?
'Yes, honesty is all there is Laura.'
'Well, there are *some* other things Thomas, but honesty is certainly high on my list.'

'Good, because I'm sure you are aware that I was married until last year.'
'Oh?' she said, a false look of surprise on her face. This was all going quite fast and being fully honest she was feeling a bit sea sick. She hadn't really expected this although she wasn't sure what she had expected. She almost had an urge to turn to Chicken and ask 'what's going on? But of course he was hundreds of miles away.
'I'm sure you've asked yourself what happened to my marriage.'
Forgetting any pretentions of honesty Laura said,
'It wouldn't have crossed my mind Thomas. It really wouldn't be any of my business.'
'Well Laura, I don't mind telling you that what destroyed my marriage was the way that I hadn't been honest with Sally from the beginning.' Curiosity kicked in for Laura.
'About your feelings you mean? Your vulnerability?'
'No Laura, about the sex. You see I have certain needs and desires. Certain preferences Laura, and Sally just couldn't come to terms with them. She was rather prudish and narrow minded. I hadn't told her about my proclivities before we were married and it came as something of a shock when I did tell her. It led to a lot of arguments and I never, never want to go through that again.' She could see that this was where she was supposed to feel sorry for him but that wasn't how she felt at all.
'Preferences?'
There was a loud rushing sound in her ears and a panic in her heart and it flashed through her mind that the hot coffee in her hand was a possible weapon.
'Yes. It's perfectly natural.'
'Are you gay?' She was really hoping he'd say yes.
'God no, I'm a red-blooded passionate heterosexual man Laura.'
'What are you talking about then?'
'Put simply, I like to be bound up. I like to be in a dark place.'
'An emotionally dark place?'

No, I don't mean emotionally, I mean literally, like a cupboard. Or a blanket box.'
'Are you taking the piss Thomas?'
'I like to be helpless Laura. For sex. It turns me on to be helpless, bound up and in a box. But Sally just couldn't see it, she was, repulsed.'
'I can't believe this. You're saying that you're into kinky sex games?'
'Not really games. Games are occasional, this is every time. I can't enjoy sex otherwise. Can you try to understand?'
Laura stood up, suddenly very sober, suddenly very aware of how ridiculous her fantasies had been. Laura's dreams hadn't involved sex at all, they'd been entirely focused on the another kind of position, a social one.
'I do understand, I fully understand Thomas and I must thank you. I think you are absolutely right. Honesty has saved us both a lot of bother. Can you call a cab for me?'
Ever the gentleman Thomas didn't even blink. He appeared to be completely unabashed.
'Of course. Laura, but will you think about it?'
'Oh, I can guarantee that I'll be thinking about it Thomas.'

It wasn't that Thomas had strange sexual tastes that shocked Laura, it was that she had somehow got herself into a situation where she was potentially a part of them. She could put up with any weirdness as long as it was at a distance, and this was a sofa seat away.

As she prepared to leave Thomas said,
'I hope you won't say anything to anyone at work about this Laura. I'm sure I can rely on your complete confidentiality.'
She turned.
'Oh, you don't understand Thomas. I actually don't have such a hang up about truth as you. It's you who will need to bite down on your honesty. I don't want ANYONE, to EVER know that I was here.'

They headed into the historic city of York on the less than ancient tarmac of the A64 and as the roadside lights flashed by Morgan said,
'The thing about TV is the size of the audience. Without it, last year in total I probably played live to eight or nine thousand people.'
'That's gigging almost every night, right?'
'Exactly. A year of hard gigging, max ten thousand people.'
'Well, that's quite a lot,' said Chicken, impressed, but Morgan only snorted.
'Ten minutes on the TV and you're reaching tens of thousands even millions. That's how to build a fan base. That's how to set yourself up for the big shows. Once you're a known face on TV you never have to worry about getting an audience again. Look at the reality show morons who build a career on it.'

The city was fast asleep and the quietness of the roads was slightly unnerving, as if they'd stumbled into a sci-fi incident, where everyone had mysteriously vanished.
'What does your friend write?' Chicken asked.
'Kevin? He wrote a successful sit-com that was on TV quite a few years ago. You'll know it, back in the 80s. It was about some blokes who work in a record company. I forget the name.'
'Hot wax?'
'YES. That's it. He made a fair bit of money, then got some other work on the back of it, even some Hollywood script consultancy stuff. But he hasn't had any kind of hit for a while so I think he makes ends meet by doing some corporate video scripts now.'
'Does he still write sit-coms?'
'Yes. He writes them, they just don't get made into shows.'
'Is he married, are we going to be making ourselves unpopular by waking up a wife and kids?'

'No. Not anymore anyhow. Kev's a nice guy but unfortunately he's one of those people who had all their success up front. It's like child star syndrome.'
'Is that a real syndrome? I never heard of it.'
'I invented it, or discovered and named it at least. It's what happens to all those screwed up showbiz kids. I mean what do you do if your best days are behind you at sixteen?'
'You go mental and take drugs.'
'Yes, or you sit trying to recapture the thing you did so easily all those years before while you live off benefits. That's Kevin, his best days are behind him but he can't let them go.'

They found Kevin's house, a large red-brick 1930s home with a drive that snaked up to it, or given that it was a short drive, wormed up to the door. There were lights on downstairs even though it was the early hours of Sunday morning and sure enough Kevin was still awake. He opened the door to them and shook Morgan's hand solemnly.
'Buddy.'
'Buddy. This is Chicken. Chicken, Kev.'
'Ah, Chicken Kiev,' he said without smiling at all, 'now we really are going to have some big fun I'll be bound.'
He was a tall but slightly over-weight man of about fifty and Chicken sensed that he wasn't the type to worry too much about the constraints of fashion. They followed him in through the door along a long hall and out the back to the kitchen. The house was untidy but not dirty, which was evidence of Kevin's employment of an efficient cleaner rather than any effort on his part. The kitchen was a large and friendly knock-through with laminate flooring throughout that made their every step clack loudly.
'A while ago I had a windfall. Two lines in a major Hollywood movie. I'm not talking lines of coke by the way, I'm talking about dialogue. My first and last. Two lines spoken by Eddie Murphy and I invested it all, every penny, in this room. That's why I bring guests in here rather than take them through to

the living room which is suffering from under-investment on an inner-city scale.'

Against the chimney breast was a white Aga cooker that was pulsing out heat. On the large pine table were three very full glasses of red wine ready poured and waiting. Morgan grabbed his greedily.

'I know you'll be tired,' said Kevin 'but I don't get many late night visitors.' He thrust a glass into Chicken's reluctant hand. 'Consider it payment to me. I mean the company that you provide tonight may give me the strength to go on tomorrow.'

'As long as you don't mind if I fall asleep in the chair.'

'Oh the chairs are far too uncomfortable for that Chicken man. You see, for all of its poise York is not a cultural city. It's a theme park tourist trap so I crave good conversation, not Americans asking me where the Minster is.'

Morgan and Kevin had met when Morgan had auditioned for a part in one of Kevin's sit-coms as it made its way through the TV production process only to fall at the pilot stage. They had kept in touch largely because Morgan liked to have somewhere free to stay when he came to York. For his part, although Kevin had plenty of experience of writing comedy he had never performed and for him there was fascination and value in hearing about what worked live from Morgan. He asked questions like,

'Why did you phrase it that way? Why did you use that word? Wouldn't it have been better if you'd said this?

He harboured the belief that if he ever did deliver his own comedy it would be exceptional, but he was also aware that without the words written down in front of him he'd never be able to remember more than a line. At one point in their relationship Kevin had offered to write some material for Morgan but Morgan had flatly refused, saying something about not being able to make other writer's jokes work for him. It had to be personal or he couldn't give it the sparkle that made it funny. Kevin felt that his writing was funny anyway, but didn't force the issue.

Chicken was feeling very tired after taking the mental beating of the gig. Watching Morgan destroy the heckler had been like having to let a big brother beat up a bully for you. It was satisfying and good entertainment, but still niggled that he hadn't been able to do it himself. And after all that doing all the driving had been a strain but now he didn't want to be rude and escape to bed. Also a big part of him thought that he should try to squeeze some rock 'n' roll living out of this trip before it was all over. Morgan was already onto his second glass of wine. Out of the corner of his eye Chicken spied a comfy looking sofa at the far end of the room, it seemed to be calling very loudly to him, telling him of its soft sponginess, so taking his glass he went to sit on it and within five minutes he was asleep.
'How was the Scarborough gig?'
'Fine, but I'm only doing these dead northern towns because my agent has arranged them as a sort of live audition with some TV people. They are going to be here in York tomorrow or is it tonight now?'
'Saturday, Sunday, whatever.'
'And what about you Kev? Busy?'
'I'm working on a film,' said Kevin. 'With a new, lottery funded production company. Exciting young director, straight out of film school.'
'Great, got a part for me?'
'It's not a comedy.'
'I could do straight acting.'
'Oh, God save us from the comedian's need to be taken seriously. We all want what we can't have don't we? The tragic human condition. You're a clown Morgan, a jester, accept your fate.'
'That's fine. It'll never get made anyway.'
Kevin took a large gulp of his wine.

'How fucking right you are Morgan. They'll tease me along, work me hard, fuck me about and then forget to call back. The same as these twats that are supposed to be coming to see your show tomorrow. Tonight. The TV people.'
'Well, I have to agree with you there Kev.' They lifted their glasses in a silent toast.

Morgan kept drinking and Kevin kept talking. He patiently told the increasingly drunken comedian about each and every project that had failed to materialise, and there were a lot of them. He told him about the near misses and almost happeneds. He told him about how he'd been existing on almost no money since the divorce and how he was having to do the dullest corporate video scripts just to stay afloat. Jobs where ignorant managing directors and marketing dicks tried to show *him* how to write. He told Morgan how much he'd come to hate the profession of comedy and about the bitterness he held towards the cruel and unlistening business of show. He told him how he'd wanted to give it all up but he didn't know what else to do other than the soul destroying video scripts. He didn't want to give up his dreams and be left knowing that company vids were his only future.
With a direct honesty born of too much alcohol, Morgan managed to slur,
'Do you think that early success screwed you up?'
'Of course it screwed me up,' yelled Kevin, 'It made me think I could do this shit and it turns out I can't. They want young.'
'They want funny,' said Morgan. 'In fact they want young AND funny.'
'I used to have both Morgan my son, and now I've got neither,' said Kevin opening another bottle of red.

SIX

As the morning streamed across the bulging duvet Laura stretched her leg out and felt the contours and expanse of an empty bed. Her main emotion was not so much sadness at the lack of Chicken, although there was definitely a touch of that, but utter relief at the absence of Thomas. When she had got back from her night out there had been another slightly garbled answer message from Chicken and she'd wanted desperately to talk to him. She lay and thought about how she would deal with Thomas on Monday. She wasn't sure. Laura was not a prude, far from it, she'd owned more than one pair of lacy knickers in her life not to mention frilly bras, but sexual deviance in men terrified her. Perhaps it was due to her strict religious upbringing and the clear moral guidelines that her mother had set out for her or maybe it was the incident when she'd innocently walked in on her uncle Shane in full gay-bondage paraphernalia. Whatever the reason anything, 'of that kind' repulsed her. For all his lack of direction and funds one thing that was true of Chicken was that he wasn't a pervert. He was an annoying shit in many ways and an infuriating dreamer and she often felt an enormous level of resentment towards the way he hadn't quite managed to grow up, and he hadn't provided a life of luxury for her, but he wasn't depraved. For one tiny second she allowed herself to imagine pretending to go along with it and then locking Thomas in a box and walking away, but violence of any kind repulsed her. It didn't make it any less awful that he would enjoy it, it made it worse.

Davis played the answer message that was causing his bedside machine to flash so insistently. He heard the digitally tinny and almost unrecognisable voice of Ray, the manager of the Grand Hotel.

'Hello, Davis. Can you tell me what's going on? Please give me a call back. I don't know what all that was about last night, but we need to have a chat. It might be worth your while.'
What the hell could he mean? Davis had not talked to him after storming off stage and then out of the club. Ray probably wanted to tell him that he owed rent or something. It was so typical. He had been right, the scheming little shit wanted to use the Grand Night's good will and reputation to launch a string of characterless comedy clubs and what made that such a painful idea was that the Grand was entirely built on Davis's efforts. AND what was more, that shit Ray didn't know great comedy when it was right there in his face. He was an idiot. Davis on the other hand was a genius but a powerless genius. He could try to start again but so much would be lost along the way.
Might be worth his while? Too many gangster films. He didn't want to talk to Ray, but he knew he'd have to, he'd left stuff at the club and he wanted it back very badly. Maybe that's what he meant? Call me back and you can have your bag. The bag had Davis's contact book in it and it was probably the most valuable and damaging thing that he could have left.

Chicken opened his eyes but couldn't move his neck. He was still in his clothes and he'd slept all night on the sofa. At some point the other two must have gone to bed and left him because the kitchen was empty. Must be recycle day, thought Chicken distractedly as his eyes passed across the table full of empty wine bottles. He felt like crap and he reminded himself why the realities of a rock 'n' roll lifestyle probably weren't for him. A night on a sofa instead of a bed had just about killed him. His original glass of wine was still untouched by his side.
Slowly Chicken got up. He stretched and groaned and eased some careful movement from his neck. He desperately needed a shower but at least he didn't have a

hangover. The terrible Scarborough gig was already fading in his mind and he was beginning to look forward to tonight in York. As he filled a glass at the sink he could hear a low rumbling noise from above that he couldn't quite put a name to. Quietly he made his way up the stairs and found the cause of the sound. In a room set up as an office Kevin was typing furiously and the force of his fingers hitting the keys on his old fashioned typewriter was the cause of the rumble.
'Morning.'
'Oh, hello. Morgan's down there in the first room but I don't think you're going to see him until much later this afternoon.'
'I see you don't believe in computers?'
'Can't work them and won't learn. Writing on a typewriter is a physical process, it's organic.'
'Sorry I fell asleep on you last night.'
'Don't worry, you missed nothing.'
'Kev, I was wondering if I could get a shower and then I'll maybe walk into the city?'
Kevin stopped typing.
'Shower by all means, go into town of course, but you must NOT visit York Minster. I forbid it.'
'Ok. Are you opposed to organised religion or something?'
'Yes, but that's not the point. I'm against tourists. I'm against people who travel with a check list of 'sites'. If you do that you are no better than a government inspector.'
'Ok. Anyway, where's the shower?'
'And I hope you aren't offended but I won't be coming to the show tonight.'
'Down at the end? The shower?'
'I hate live comedy. Can't stand it. Ask yourself Chicken, if you weren't performing would you go to comedy clubs? Would you pay to sit with students who know nothing of real life and who laugh at swear words?'
It was a good question and later as Chicken stood under a wonderfully warm jet of water he found himself answering no. He wouldn't choose to spend his leisure time in a

comedy venue which led to the obvious follow up question; why was he doing it now?

After he'd showered and changed clothes Chicken went back to ask Kevin if he could use the phone.

'Of course, but the only one I've got is here.' It was next to Kevin on the desk. 'Thanks, I need to call my wife. We haven't had much contact since Thursday.'

'Be my guest, but I'm afraid I can't stop working, I'm pursuing a train of thought and I can't let it escape.'

Chicken reached and picked up the phone from beside Kevin. He didn't really want to have this conversation in front of him, but it seemed that he had no choice.

'Hello?'

'Blimey, you're in.'

'Why wouldn't I be, it's Sunday morning. It's you who isn't in.'

'No, I just meant that I've tried to get hold of you a couple of times and you were out. Did you get my messages?'

'Yes. Anyway, how's it going?'

'Really good. Scarborough last night, and now we're staying here in York where our last gig is.'

'What's that noise?'

'Noise? Oh that's Kevin. He's right here with me and he's typing.'

'Typing?'

'He's a famous writer,' he looked at Kevin to give him a knowing wink but he was focused on his machine.

'I'm looking forward to you getting home.'

'Me too.'

'Miss you.'

'Miss you too.'

When he'd finished his call, Kevin who was still staring intently at his page asked,

'So how does your wife feel about your life in the lower bowels of comedy?'

'Um, she's pretty impressed I'd say.'

'Mine was too, in the beginning, until the money stopped

rolling in. She found it hard to see the artistic integrity of writing jokes when she couldn't buy food anymore.'
'Well, Laura earns enough to buy her own food, and fortunately most of mine too.'
Kevin looked sideways at him before answering.
'Well, Chicken, I'm sure that arrangement isn't the cause of any marital conflict.'

The road that led into town was wide and leafy and ran alongside a large racecourse. Chicken stopped to read a plaque that informed him that Dick Turpin had been hanged on that site. Might be worth a mention later on stage, he thought, hanging was always a good subject for comedy. As he walked he started to mentally go over his act. He was looking forward to getting back out there and putting things right. He wasn't afraid, he'd done enough gigs to know that it was an unpredictable rollercoaster. He also knew he could do much better than he'd done in Scarborough, especially if he stayed away from alcohol.
At the edge of the city he found a gate that led up onto the old city walls. He knew it was probably forbidden by Kevin, but when he saw that entry was free he defiantly went up the ancient stone steps. The walkways were busy with Chinese tourists, and they had open travel books so presumably had more idea than him as to what there was to see. He followed a group. They looked like they knew where they were going which was more than he did.
It was like being on the parapet of a castle. At some parts of the walls he could see down into people's gardens, and saw their brightly coloured plastic swings and slides and their rusting barbeque sets. It brought up the familiar thoughts that he always had when he got a secret glimpse of other people's lives. How did they come to be there? What did they do? What was it like living there? Could he do it? How did they manage to survive this far from London?
The forbidden Minster was in sight for almost all of his walk, a big old church that dominated the skyline and though it

certainly was on the tourist trail, Kev would not have had to ban Chicken from visiting it. Chicken had no interest at all in churches of any size or age. The Chinese party who were still walking in front of Chicken were very excited to be nearing it and Chicken sniggered to think that they really knew the meaning of things that were forbidden. He let that turns in his mind and wondered if he could get a joke out of it by the time they went to the club. In the past some of Chicken's last minute observations had worked quite well and he always liked the feeling of doing something fresh.

By the time Chicken made his way back to the house he was exhausted. He'd enjoyed his ramble, but it had struck him as very odd to be alone and he'd felt completely removed from normal life. It wasn't a holiday and it wasn't business, it was some strange limbo land that he was inhabiting and he was starting to dislike it. Laura would have really liked it in York, and knowing that made him feel quite uneasy.
Morgan was out of his bed and up drinking coffee in the kitchen and he barely nodded when Chicken came in.
Above them the rumbling continued. Chicken made himself a cup of tea.
'I think he's lost it,' he said pointing towards the ceiling.
'He's always been like that. Obsessed.'
'And mental?'
'Only a touch.'

The Starlight Club in York was located in the basement of an arts centre and cinema in the centre of the city. In true wild-man style they took a bus into town, an over long purple bendy thing that struggled to negotiate the sharp turns designed for a long past age. Morgan was excited and was bubbling with chat.
'Love this gig. Always a good one.'
The comedians approached the club by walking along a fairly ordinary car-free main shopping street and then suddenly taking a left turn through a narrow gap next to a

church. Another world seemed to open up. The building overlooked the river and was one of the nicest looking venues that Chicken had encountered. On seeing it he immediately thought of The Black Swan in Deptford, which also sat next to water but was at the other end of the beauty scale. The Black Swan wasn't even a charming dump, it had nothing going for it except the most aggressive and nasty crowd on the circuit. No, this was the place to be, the glamorous Starlight.

From the second they stepped through the automatic doors Chicken felt good, the place was buzzing with trendy middle-class people. Not all of them were here for the comedy, some had just come out of one of the films and were in animated discussion about the merits of Japanese cinema. They were here for a good time and Chicken was going to do his best to give it to them. As they made their way towards the stairs Chicken studied the faces. He passed. Someone here was a TV exec, and for the first time Chicken could really believe it, in fact he wouldn't have been surprised if they'd all been TV producers with their modern haircuts and canvas shoulder bags. Of course they were they were to see Morgan, but it couldn't do Chicken any harm to put in a good gig. The possibility of recognition was what he'd sold Laura on to get here, so all he needed was a positive email from someone with an impressive email address to show that he was moving in the right direction.

They walked down the open plan steel and wood stairs and through a door into the basement bar.

'We're not open yet,' said a man stacking glasses behind the bar.

'We're comedians.'

'Oh, right, Sean's in the green room through that way.'

Green room? Thought Chicken, have I actually made it? They have a green room.

The basement had a low ceiling which gave it a lovely intimate feel. Chicken followed Morgan past the tables and through a door behind the stage which took them into a room that was surprisingly enormous. The space was equivalent to the size of the rest of the club. There was a drum kit right in the middle, left there by a band that hired out the place for practice and various boxes of theatrical props.

'Wow, this is some green room. It's like a green aircraft hangar,' said Chicken agog.

Standing at a sound system presumably organising the music for the show was a young guy Chicken knew to be Sean O'Farrel, a headlining comedian in his own right. Sean had come up from London that day to compere the gig and he'd travelled up with Marcia Craig, one of the very rare women on the circuit, who was now sitting quietly reading. Marcia had TV credits and a big reputation which she had painstakingly earned with razor sharp one-liners and laser hot observations. Chicken was in great company and it was slightly intimidating but he was feeling quite confident for a change. Even the need to visit the toilet had abated. It was a good sign.

Morgan of course knew both of the others and immediately fell into conversation as if he'd been there all day. The latest gossip was of a comedian who had been busted by the tax office after a 30 year career of cash in hand.

'You've got to have an accountant,' Marcia was saying, 'If you're a professional you've got to do it right.'

'I've got one,' admitted Morgan, 'but in my defence he's shit.'

Sean finished with the music and went through the running order.

'So it's me, then a short break, then me, then Marcia, then a break then me then you.'

Morgan nodded,

'Fine, I'll do 45 to 50.'

Chicken waited for Morgan to add him to the line-up but nothing happened, so he coughed in a theatrically noticeable way. Morgan picked up the hint,

'Oh yes, can Chicken here have a 10 minute open?'

Sean squinted at Chicken and shook his head.

'Sorry mate, no can do. The club has a policy of no opens. They only book professionals.'
'He is a professional. Can we squeeze him in?'
'Not possible I'm afraid Morgan. The management are in, they would feed it back to the booking agency and we wouldn't get a chance to come back again. Plus, you know what they're like, we might not get paid.'
Chicken couldn't believe what he was hearing, but he now expected Morgan to exert some real pressure the way he had in Scarborough. This time it didn't happen, instead Morgan shrugged and said,
'Fair enough.'
Chicken pulled him roughly to one side, there was plenty of room in the green room for that.
'Fair enough? What the fuck do you mean, fair enough? You know what I've been through to be here tonight. This is my chance to put aside last night, like you told me, on to the next, right?'
'Look, I'm really sorry Chicken but there's nothing I can do.'
'You could walk out like you said you would last night.'
'No, not tonight. This gig has become the reason for the whole fucking trip mate, and I'm not bailing now. They are out there. I can't threaten to walk, he might take me at my word. Sean would love to do the whole night himself. AND he'd probably get a TV show out of it. My TV show.'
'What about me Morgan?'
'I'll get you a gig when we get back to London. At the Windmill. Biggest gig in South London.'
'Tonight. What about me tonight?'
'Get a beer, enjoy the show.'
'Are you off your trolley? I have driven you all over the fucking north of England. I don't want to watch the show, I want to be the show.'
'What can I say, it's not my call bud.'

Chicken took a deep breath and glanced around the green room. Sean and Marcia were deliberately and conspicuously occupied with other things and he could see he wasn't going to get any support. He squared his shoulders.

'Have a great gig Morgan. I'm off.'

He turned and walked back out past the stage and the rapidly filling tables, up past the bar, he pushed past the queue at the door and on out into the night. Built at the back of the cinema was a very contemporary decking area suspended above the river like the side of a ship. Raging with anger Chicken went over to the rail to watch the dark water flowing past twenty feet below.

'What a twat,' he said aloud. How was he going to explain this to Laura? How was he going to explain it to himself? He desperately wanted to blame Morgan but he knew deep down that the blame really lay at his own door. Who was it who had been stupid enough to join this crazy train? To even volunteer to drive the friggin train.

His legs were still aching a bit from his afternoon of sauntering round the walls of York but he set off on foot to go back to Kevin's house to pick up the car. Away from the quiet side street that housed the club, gangs of hen-party women dressed in identical pink sashes and other hilarious store bought costume accessories were screeching and lurching through the streets. Chicken began to weave and stutter his route in order to avoid the worst of them. There was something very painful in having to witness such blatant funning and jollity when all he wanted to do was cry the bitter tears of a six year old dropped from the school nativity play. As he walked he shook his head every few minutes at the injustice of it. How hard would it have been to let him on for ten minutes? Even five minutes.

Back at the house Chicken entered through the kitchen and shouted up the stairs that he wasn't a burglar. The typewriter's rumble ceased and Kevin came down surprised to see his guest return so early. When he learned what had happened he showed a touchingly genuine concern.

'God, I'm sorry to hear that. That's really bad man. What a bunch of tits. I don't understand why they did that. It's not

Sunday Night at the London Palladium? It's a comedy club in the basement of a fucking York cinema?' he sighed heavily. 'But they are selfish people Chicken, comedians are very selfish, self-absorbed, damaged people and you can't expect any real humanity.'
The sympathy was starting to make Chicken feel uncomfortable.
'Yeah, well anyway thanks for putting us up Kevin. I've got a wife to get back to so I'm going to get going.' They shook hands in some kind of formal acknowledgement of Chicken's terrible loss.
'Are you going to leave Morgan here to find his own way back?'
'I really thought about it Kev, but while I was walking I was thinking and I decided no, I'm going to meet him when he comes out. I brought him so I'll take him back.'
'That's nice of you Chicken. I know it wasn't really his fault but he could have put up a bigger fight after you've driven him so many miles. And you know it says something about who you are. Even though they are the selfish ones it shows why you are different from them. Why you are better than them.'
'Yes. It also shows that he owes me money Kev, and if I don't get it tonight I doubt if I'll ever get it.'

Morgan stepped from the door of the club and Chicken shouted to him from the end of the street where he was waiting with the car. As soon as he jumped in Morgan pointed at the road ahead.
'Straight back to London my man.'
As they swapped the city lights for the lights of the motorway, Morgan said,
'It was a massive shame.' Chicken nodded in silent agreement in the dark of the car. Morgan continued, 'I mean they were a great crowd, they were ready for anything so it was such a shame that I didn't get to do my speed dating material.' Chicken turned to look at him. 'Marcia had

already done a whole bit on speed dating and I couldn't risk sounding derivative especially with the TV people there. You should have seen it, I killed them with the man boob stuff though. Killed 'em. I can't guarantee that they were there, not based on my stupid agent, but if they were that's a TV show in the bag.'

Morgan's tongue had been loosened by the heady mixture of triumph and alcohol. For the next hour or so Chicken listened to how brilliantly the gig had gone with a sense of disbelief and growing resentment and anger. On the M1 not far past Sheffield the Mitsubishi began to judder and lurch until it limped into the hard shoulder. They sat wordlessly for ten minutes. Eventually Morgan said,

'Is this a problem?'

Chicken did not like talking about money, especially money he was owed and he never had. For some inexplicable reason, perhaps caused by some now forgotten childhood incident involving sweets and pocket money, or a deeply buried socialist instinct that made money a dirty word, the whole subject embarrassed him. It certainly had something to do with his self-image. He didn't like to come across as greedy or mean and he didn't want to leave an impression that mere money was a subject that ruled his life. For a person who was willing to stand up in front of strangers and discuss his early sexual experiences for laughs it was bizarre that he couldn't talk about cash, not even with Laura. It made any attempts to control his personal finances very difficult. In the course of his life, from the playground to his self-employed graphic design business he had often been taken advantage of by those who have no problem with not paying up. It was a sign of just how pissed off he was with the northern tour that he was now prepared to be a grown up.

'Morgan, you owe me some money.'

'Right, well, can we sort all that out when we...' Chicken was not in the mood to negotiate. He was not prepared to finance

a trip that he'd got nothing out of except the chance to be humiliated, the possible loss of his freelance work and marriage.
'No, I know you've just been paid at the end of that gig and I want to be paid the petrol money and the money I spent on my credit card. You owe me a hundred and sixty quid. If I'm the driver Morgan, then I get paid.'
'Look, chill out fella, it's only money. You'll get paid...'
'I want to be paid now, Morgan.' The look he now gave Morgan told him very clearly that whatever else this statement was, it certainly wasn't a joke. Morgan sighed and reached into his pocket.
'It's come to this, bitching over a few quid.' He shuffled through a large roll of cash and counted out the money. 'There's your money Chicken, and I'm paying in advance because as it stands you haven't got me home yet.'

Chicken borrowed Morgan's mobile phone. First he rang Laura and told her that they were likely to be very late, that she shouldn't worry and that she might not see him before she went to work. And then he rang the AA to find that it would be at least an hour's wait before anyone could get to them. They sat in the desolate lane the Mitsy rocking slightly with every car or lorry that whined past. They had been told to get out of the car for safety reasons, but they ignored that advice on the petulant basis that they didn't want to. Recognising that there was something of an atmosphere Morgan rubbed his tired eyes.
'You had a good gig in Hull,' he said at last to break the silence.
'Thanks.'
'The only way you can get better is to do loads of gigs.'
'I know.'
'You've got to put in your ten thousand hours.'
'I know. I tried to do one more in York, remember?'
'Do you want any advice? Not everyone wants it.'
'Shoot.'

'You've got good material, a lot of it's better than mine. You're a good writer. But there are some people who have great jokes, but they are not funny people.'
'I'm not funny?'
'To paraphrase an old saying, some comedians say funny things and some say things funny. Tommy Cooper could have read the phonebook and it would have been funny.'
'And that's not me?'
'No.'
'So what does that mean? I should give up?'
'No, the opposite. You have to keep going until you've built up enough confidence to deliver your jokes properly every time. You have to be able to let go a little more. You've got to...perform. Entertain.'
The analysis wasn't what Chicken wanted to hear at all. He wanted to hear that he was a comedy genius waiting to be discovered but what hurt the most was knowing that Morgan was right. He couldn't quite let go up under the lights.
'And what about you Morgan?'
'I make a reasonable living, and it's a lifestyle that I like.'
'But by the time he was your age Billy Connolly had conquered the world. If you can't be Billy, if you don't have that raw talent what's the point?'
'The point is that I can't do anything else. I have no other skills. This is me. This is what I do. And if this TV thing works out I'll be making good money at last. Anyway, who's Billy Connolly? Did he used to be funny?'
'Not sure, but who's Tommy Cooper? Did he used to be alive?'
Chicken had thought that when the AA eventually arrived they might need to be relayed all the way home, which as he wouldn't have had to drive would have been his preference. The flashing yellow lights of the truck were oddly comforting, a bright reminder that someone who knew what they were doing had arrived. After thirty minutes of tinkering the mechanic had managed to get the old Mitsubishi going. The technical explanations of their breakdown were lost on

Chicken but he did pick up the advice that as soon as he got back to London he should get his car to a garage. Or a breaker's yard. Whatever had kept them sitting by the side of the road was a terminal disease as far as the Mitsy was concerned. It was yet another piece of great news that he'd have to deliver to Laura when he got back after she'd spent a weekend sitting in on her own watching the telly. Mind you, when he thought about it she had been out somewhere because she hadn't answered the phone. That would mean him having to feign interest in some boring story of a wacky solicitors knees-up no doubt.

'I'm not paying for a new car,' Morgan said, as they pulled back into the thin early hours traffic. 'And I'm thinking that I should be getting a discount on this delayed journey.'

'Fuck off.'

'Now, you see, that's how to deal with a heckler, Chicken.'

SEVEN

When you're really not trying to be early, how come you can't help being ahead of schedule? thought Laura sitting at the kitchen table sipping a cup of tea. She was fully dressed and made up in her hard-hitting corporate style, her leather briefcase shining on the floor beside her. She took in the subtle evidence of Chicken's existence around her, his dirty shoes by the back door (slob), his phone charger on the side (idiot), his special jar of mixed pickle on top of the fridge having not quite made it inside (lazy, slobbish, idiot). She was disappointed not to have seen him this morning and she had been lagging in her rituals and preparation half in the hope that he would get back, but as yet there was no sight. The other half of her reason for taking her time was the wish to avoid Thomas Dalfin. They had got into the habit of meeting on the train into work to share a few laughs and work gossip and she was keen to stop that now. It wasn't so much that she was shocked at Thomas, after all, all men were little more than dogs, it was more that she was ashamed of how dazzled she'd allowed herself to become, so quickly. She'd had a narrow escape, she knew it, and now she wanted to draw a line under it. There was no need to socialise with Thomas, she hadn't done before the briefcase incident and she now wanted to put that particular genie back in its bottle. Her plan was to avoid talking to him on the morning journey, limit her email contact with him and make sure that she was always busy for lunch. She was certain that it would suit both of them, surely beneath his upper-class insouciance there was a shred of embarrassment.
She checked the clock, she couldn't delay any longer, so with a heavy sigh she set off for the tube.
Perhaps Thomas had been attempting the same avoidance plan but when the later train pulled in, he was on it and before she could turn away he'd caught her eye. There was

no easy escape other than turning and running. She got on. There were no seats so they stood swaying and carried out a more stilted than usual morning conversation. Off the train at last and walking to the office at a fairly cracking pace Thomas asked the only question that hinted at any personal subject.
'Is your husband back from his business trip?' She assessed the question before answering.
'He will be back today.'
'Good. That's nice. What is it he does again? I don't think you said?'
'He's with Back, Sack and Crack,' she giggled and then added, 'He's a comedian.' For once Laura felt a tinge of pride when she said it. Wrapped up in that statement were all kinds of things like, he doesn't do what everyone else does, he's not boring, he's very brave and he's almost a celebrity.
'A what?'
'A comedian. He goes around the country spreading happiness and making people laugh.'
'God, how awful.' Thomas's breeding took over from his instinct and he quickly stopped himself from saying much more. 'I mean to have to do so much travelling. And it must be so nerve wracking. In working men's clubs and things.' Laura could see how unacceptable someone being an entertainer was to Thomas, how low class and cheap. She suddenly felt quite proud of Chicken.

When Laura got into the office her PA was already at her desk typing away busily as usual. The seminar that was coming up needed a lot of work and because Laura had been rather distracted of late Elizabeth had stepped into the breach. Laura often wondered why Elizabeth didn't leave and get a well paid Marketing Manager job herself. Perhaps she was waiting for Laura's role, but given that Laura was a non-smoking, clean living bore she might have to wait a while for a heart attack to promote her. Elizabeth could

probably be quite effective if she was a little more pro-active and ruthless. In the male dominated legal profession if she used that incredible shape that she kept well hidden with understated outfits she'd be unstoppable.
After their customary round of, Good weekend? You? Elizabeth asked,
'So how was the big fancy meal?'
'Fine, fine. Very nice.'
'How was Thomas?' It was said in a flat, unchallenging way that was loaded with curiosity.
'I'll be honest Elizabeth, all I can say is don't get into any social situations with him unless you have a very broad mind.'
'You mean he's a letch?'
'Kind of. I can't really talk about it Elizabeth, but all I will say is he has some very strange habits.'
'Like what? You can't leave me hanging with that!'
'I'm afraid I'll have to, you wouldn't want to know. Now listen Elizabeth, little research job for you. Will you please find me everything there is on the internet about my husband and his comedy, please?'
'Like his profile on uk comedians? Like his gig list from last year? Like some of the better reviews?'
'Yes, I suppose so. Anything really?'
'It won't take long, I've got a lot of that stuff on my favourites. What's this about?'
'I just think it's time I showed a little interest in my husband's interests that's all.'
'So how was his big northern tour?'
'He's not back yet. They had some sort of car problem but I can't wait to hear all about it tonight.'
Elizabeth was absolutely burning with curiosity about Thomas now, but she could tell that she wasn't going to get any more from Laura. Instead she'd have to use her own powers of investigation. Thomas had acted very strangely that time he'd followed her into the tiny stationery store cupboard, perhaps he had OCD or was claustrophobic?

He returned from his sister's house in Scarborough after the glorious purging of his soul through the religious cleansing medium of 'heckle' with a new crystal clear purpose and belief. Jane had been right on all counts. Yes, comedy meant a lot to him, perhaps more than it should and yes, he'd only given it one go.

Danny walked into his office with a real spring in his step and after an hour of sorting out work emails and some paperwork he booked a meeting room for himself, closed the blinds and began working on his plan. He had read in a self-help book that for a plan to work you had to write it down, so he mapped it out on a pad. He wrote 1. The Act. First he needed to write some funny material, short punchy jokes. Get to the laughs quickly. He needed to have a really strong opening and then a good solid middle and a very funny finale. He'd noticed that a lot of comedians used a self-effacing start to their act. Get the audience laughing at you, make them realise that you don't think you're better than them, and then they will accept you. Then he wrote 2. Rehearse. He couldn't risk not knowing what to say next, and he couldn't rely on thinking things up on the spur of the moment. So, once he'd written his act, then he'd practice. 3. Get gig only when I'm ready. Danny wasn't going to go back to the club where he'd crashed and burned, but there were plenty of others. Point four was 'ignore any criticism, just keep going.' This was the key. He had a strong feeling that no gig could ever be as bad as that first one. It had been his baptism of fire. Fire laced with acid and razor blades. He'd lived through it so he knew he was going to be ok.

There was a knock at the office door and Jonathan put his head in.

'Oh, hi, I know you've booked it, but do you really need the room? We're out here waiting for the 11 o'clock slot and...'

'Yes, I need it Jon, otherwise I wouldn't be here.'

'I just thought maybe the others hadn't turned up?'

'Oh, right like I'd been stood up?'

'Well, that they had been too busy perhaps.'
'It's a planning meeting Dom. Personal development and a major part of this company's focus for all of us so I need total quiet to concentrate.'
Jon sheepishly said sorry and ducked out. Danny checked over his pad. It was all there, now all he had to do was write the act. He began to write a line, scribble it out and then write it again. After twenty minutes he had a page full of crossings out and one weak joke that played on the fact that he looked a bit like a skinny version of Robbie Coltrane. It wasn't going to be easy, but he wasn't going to give up. When he left the meeting room at eleven he passed the colleagues who were waiting to go in, his pad under his arm. He marched past briskly. Little did they know how personally developed he was going to be once the plan had come to fruition.

The chilling North Eastern sea breeze of Scarborough was rolling along the seafront but on this Monday morning in November there were very few tourists to be enticed into the arcades. It was just as well because most of the arcades were shuttered anyway. Being a hotel, albeit a quiet one at this time of the year, the Grand Hotel was open of course and Davis breezed through and down to the basement in search of his bag. When he couldn't find it he asked at the desk and was directed to Ray's office. He'd wanted to avoid having to speak to the manager but he wasn't going to get a choice if he wanted his bag back. In such circumstances it was always best to take a high line he'd found, to be confident and aggressive and not back down. He certainly wasn't going to apologise for the show that Morgan had put on, it was awesome and as far as he was concerned it was the reason the crowd would keep on coming back. Ok, so a few oldsters might get offended, but really, who needed them?
He was ushered through to Ray's room and then asked to sit down, while Ray finished a phone call. The girl who had

done the ushering then came in with a small tray with two cups of coffee, a small jug of milk and two individually wrapped oat biscuits. Ray was still on the phone talking about laundry deliveries so Davis ate both of the biscuits. He wasn't quite sure what was going on. Was he being softened up before being bumped off? Was he in a bad gangster movie?

Eventually Ray put the phone down. He held out his hand to shake. Uncomfortably Davis shook it.

'So, Davis, let's put Sunday night behind us because I think you've been getting the wrong end of the stick.'

'Sure Ray. By the way do you have my bag, I left it here.'

Ray reached below his desk, rolled open a drawer, pulled out the ratty bag and handed it across.

'I locked it in my office, I didn't want it going walkies.' Davis opened the zip to see that his contact book was still there and was relieved to pick it out.

'Did you look in here?' Ray frowned, insulted.

'I wouldn't go through your private property Davis, what do you think I am?'

'Ok,' it sounded like the sort of thing that people say when they've been through your things to Davis.

'Look Davis, you don't seem to trust me so let me just ask what I'm going to ask. That way if you aren't interested we can go our separate ways.'

Separate ways? Davis was about to launch into an hysterical diatribe on how he had made the club what it was, how he'd sweated blood, how he'd given it the best years of his life, how it was now going to be abused by a moron like him, but fortunately Ray got in first saving him the embarrassment.

'Davis, I like what you've done with this comedy club. You've made it what it is. Even though I don't approve of all of the material that I've heard I can see that your energy and enthusiasm has kept the place alive. You have the valuable contacts.' I do now, thought Davis cradling the bag.

'I don't know if you know about our empire Davis? We're part of a leisure chain. We have hotels in Bridlington, Filey,

Scarborough and even one way up in Saltburn. In short Davis, I'd like to see a comedy club in each of those venues, playing to the locals during the winter and to the tourists during the summer. I want to be able to offer food and refreshments like those comedy places down in London. I want to have a stranglehold on east coast comedy.' He rose from behind his desk to stare moodily from the window. Outside rain was sheeting along the road. Davis could not see where this was going but he had an inkling and thought it best to keep quiet and let him roll.
'I know it's hard to get the best London comedians to come up here Davis, but if they're coming up for four guaranteed gigs on consecutive nights, PLUS cheap hotel accommodation it might be worth their while?'
'Might be. Will I still be running the Scarborough gig?'
'What I'm proposing Davis is that you would run all the clubs.'
'All of them?'
'Yes, it would be a paid position and I can't think of a better person to do it. We'd pay you on a retainer, like a freelance entertainment officer, and you'd also get a percentage of the door. That would be your incentive to make sure the places stayed full.'
Davis wanted to run round the office shouting 'yes, at last' but all he could think to say was,
'Would I get free drinks on gig night?'
'Of course, as long as you stayed sober. Which brings me to my next point. I know you have comedy ethics and a radical view of pure comedy, but I want to attract an older audience. Frankly in this area there are more of them. I want those retired clubs and the like as regulars. So we need you to use your experience, knowledge and contacts to only book comedians that can play to a more reserved crowd. An older audience.'
'You mean not potty mouths like Morgan?'
'Exactly.'

Davis had been flattered, buttered up and bribed. He'd been sewn up.

'I think that's exactly where my strength lies,' he said, 'knowing the acts.' Besides, he thought, Morgan was a bit over the top, and it was only entertainment. It's only supposed to be a bit of a laugh. Give the people what they want.

Chicken let himself into the house knowing that Laura would have already left for work but he dumped his bag and shouted up the stairs just in case. She didn't reply and he was slightly glad about that. He wasn't ready for her yet, he was exhausted. They had stopped in a lay-by for a little while so that he could try to sleep, but it hadn't really worked out. Sleeping in a car is much more uncomfortable than it should be. Instead of rest, when they stopped to fill up with petrol they also tanked up on Redbull.

It was the slowest, most arduous trip he'd ever taken and when he'd eventually dropped Morgan off at the first Northern Line station they'd reached it had been an awkward goodbye. They were both too tired to say very much. Chicken had muttered something about letting him know how the TV thing worked out and Morgan had said he would and then mumbled that he'd be in touch with some gigs for Chicken who said thanks knowing that it would never happen.

The house was quiet and he wondered if he should check his emails to see if any work had come in. The thought paralysed him. He looked at the silent, black screened Apple Mac in the kitchen and it stabbed some guilt into his heart. He was in a bit of an over-tired trance walking from room to room seeing if anything had changed. In the lounge he picked up microphone that he used for practice, almost said his opening line, but then thought better of it and put it down again.

He didn't know whether to eat, drink or sleep, and decided to shed his clothes and climb under the beautifully cool duvet.

He should have showered first, and he could almost hear Laura's voice saying so. He should have dropped straight into a coma, but lay staring at the wall. What had he just done? What had he gained from the whole episode except a broken car and more questions than answers. You should never give up, but at what point is it just plain stupid to keep going? He wasn't progressing. He had a handful of gigs that he could perform at, but it wasn't growing and he wasn't sure that he was getting any better. Meanwhile his student-like life could not continue. Soon, very soon, perhaps even already, Laura would tire of the way he was not achieving anything and he'd be out. He was now thirty-three, so if it took another seven years he'd be forty, and comedians just didn't break through at forty. Sure, they could carry on building on a fan base that they already had at forty, they could tour and make DVDs at forty, but they couldn't convince students that they had any relevance or cred at forty. Twenty was a good breakthrough age, maybe twenty five and as fatigue confused as Chicken was he still knew twenty was about half of forty.

For the first time in days he thought about the future of his freelance design work and it sent a squirmy bullet of fear to his heart. The truth was that he had nothing coming in, nothing. There would be no money for his half of the mortgage by next month. The hundred odd pounds in his pocket was not going to solve any problems. What he needed was a lottery win, and as he drifted off to sleep a plan comforted him. Buy a ticket.

Chicken awoke to find Laura standing over him with a cup of tea, she was smiling. He'd slept all day and he now sat up groggily. She leaned over and gave him a kiss.

'So how did it go?' he knew that the thing to do with Laura was only to tell her good news, bad news sent her into an equally bad mood. She had to be protected from the little downs on life's highway and completely isolated from the major potholes and road works. She often had a crisis of

perspective as far as Chicken was concerned blowing things out of proportion and seeing catastrophe where only setbacks existed. But now, in his half asleep state he really didn't have the energy to find the sugar to coat the pill and he wasn't sharp enough to think through the consequences.
'Disastrously,' he said. She looked disappointed.
'What do you mean?'
'I didn't get to perform last night. They wouldn't let me because I wasn't on the original bill.'
'You drove all the way to York and they didn't let you play?'
Normally Chicken would have found excuses, but not this evening.
'That's right. And then the car broke down on the way back. It's going to need work. Expensive work. Or maybe the scrap yard. And I came away with no money. I covered costs, which actually makes a change for me, but I didn't make any profit.'
Ominously, at first she didn't say anything at all. She was nodding slowly, then she said, 'You poor thing, you must have been gutted.'
'About the car?'
'No, about not getting the gig.'
'Yes, I was. More than gutted really.' She rubbed his shoulder.
'Were there any high points?'
'Hull. Hull was excellent. That was the first one, but it was downhill from there.' He swigged the tea. 'What about you? Did you have a nice weekend?'
'Well, there was a firm dinner on Saturday night. Corporate. Boring. You'd have hated it. Other than that I missed you really.'
Laura had decided long ago that honesty was not the best policy in the politics of marriage. As she saw it there was nothing to tell anyway so there was nothing to be gained by saying it. She knew that nothing ever would have happened with Thomas so there was no reason to open that can of

snakes. Besides it sounded like Chicken wasn't ready for any more hits.

'So what about the TV thing you mentioned?'

'Forget it.'

Elizabeth's internet research had shown Laura that although her PA was excited at every blog mention and forum name check, Chicken was hardly setting the web alight.

'So what will you do Chicken? What's going to happen?' He could hear the panic and anger rising in her voice. He thought about the lottery and it made him smile to think about throwing that in as a solution.

'Well, if it's not too late to rescue I'm going to get hold of your mate Katy at Zingtastic. It's time I got a real job Laura, this student lifestyle is getting me nowhere.' She gave a wide smile and Chicken could tell that he'd pulled it out of the fire, for now.

'Well, you have given it a go haven't you? And I think if you were going to make it you'd have done it by now.'

'You think?'

'Oh, yes. Maybe this whole trip or tour or whatever it was was the best thing for you, it showed you the truth.'

'That I'm crap?'

'No. That perhaps it isn't for you.'

Chicken closed his eyes and lay down. He visualised walking out in Hull. The jokes that went so well, the guy in the shell suit afterwards telling him that he was funny. The look of respect from Morgan.

Laura watched over Chicken as he lay with his eyes closed and she found herself wondering if he ever wanted to be locked in a box for sex. Men were strange.

EIGHT

Morgan met Matty Carlo in the Rose and Crown in Soho amongst the assorted media types, wanna-bees, might have beens and other daytime drinkers. There were always some famous faces that you couldn't quite place. Matty did have a proper office nearby with a water cooler, over-flowing desk, harassed secretary and a leather sofa but Morgan didn't like going there. At least this way he got a couple of drinks out of the leech. Like most artists Morgan resented every penny that he paid to Matty for every booking that he knew he would have got anyway. Some people were able to rationalise the fifteen to twenty percent they paid as better than the nothing that they would have without an agent. Morgan was not one of them. The yoghurt ad was done, spent and forgotten.
They sat at a table, Matty in his suit jacket and open pink shirt, Morgan in his blue T-shirt, today bearing the slogan AWOL.
'So, they were there, they saw me work, what did they think?'
Matty did not answer immediately, he wanted to squeeze his power for just a few more seconds and paused like a reality show host announcing an eviction. At last he said,
'Yes, the good news is that Mike and Peter, from Upchuck Productions, were at your gig in York Morgan.'
'Cool.'
'Yes. But not that cool Morgan because it was quite difficult to convince them that they should go. I had to work very, very hard.' Morgan snorted at Matty's blatant and rather pathetic attempt to justify his fee.
'Oh, really? Why?'
'Because they were also at the gig in Scarborough the night before, where I believe you gave a master-class in obnoxious ranting.'
Morgan sat back on his seat and drank some lager.

'They saw that?'
'Yes.'
'It was funny, everyone said so. I handled a situation. That heckler was a God send.'
'It may have been funny Morgan but would you say it was mainstream TV audience fodder?'
'Who gives a fuck? Probably not. But they saw York, right? I was mister entertainment in York. I was mainstream all the way to the bank. I was so middle of the road they could have painted a white line on me.'
'That's right. They liked York so I had to explain to them how these things go sometimes.'
'You had to explain to them? Do they know anything at all about comedy?'
'They make comedy TV shows Morgan, of course they don't know anything about comedy.' They both laughed at that.
'So what happens next? What do they have for me?'
'Ok, they think you've got great potential for TV. They see a developing career.'
'Fantastic.'
'But you need a vehicle to get you rolling in the public eye. There's only a tiny fraction of the population that ever goes to a comedy club we all know that.'
'These are all the things that I've been saying to you for years Matty. You're telling me things that I have been telling you. Now you listen because it's them. So, what do they have for me?'
'Have you heard of Chazbatz?' Morgan just blinked. He didn't even take a drink, he simply blinked. Everyone had heard of Chazbatz, it was the biggest show of its genre, and boasted a massive audience. But the audience was only big in number not in actual size because Chazbatz was a wacky knock-about comedy show for pre-school kids.
'Now I know what you're thinking Morgan.'
'You don't.'
'It's a kids show, but you've got to see the big picture. You're on national TV, the show is watched by sexy moms and

students. They get high and freak out to that show. The students I mean. When you get to a live gig, they know you from the show, you go out and do adult humour like you do and they love it. It makes you a cult. Meanwhile you're earning your stripes as a TV performer before you move on to the big stuff. And more importantly for you, you're also earning money. It pays.'

'You mean I'll be earning you some percentage.'

'Don't be cynical Morgan. I've never known a comedian be cynical before.'

There was a lot of truth in what Matty was saying about the show but it wasn't the point. Kids programmes probably did pay well but they were a trap. In the same way that porn stars never broke into mainstream film acting kids' entertainers never made it into real comedy. It just didn't happen, and Morgan didn't need the student gig boost, he was doing fine at that anyway. Morgan didn't trust Matty's agenda and Matty was pushing on.

'You do a season as the friendly bin-man, that's the part, the last one's getting dropped over some cocaine scandal that's about to hit the rags. You take over, get your name out there and then we move you up the ladder later.'

'Matty, as my father used to say, I'm disappointed. Shall I tell you how I saw it? My own comedy show. With writers. A budget and a good production team. I've got loads of ideas. Sketches and stand-up. If not that maybe a sit-com, something cool and funny. Even a show like Smartarse Challenge where I could make my way into the hearts of the nation.'

Matty nodded excitedly.

'This is what I'm saying Morgan, this is how those things start.'

'No they don't,' he said standing up, 'This is how they end. Kids shows is where you go when you've shot your bolt and it's all there is left.' He leaned over the table to get close to Matty's face.

'Harry Fuckin' Steadford didn't start in kids shows, and he's not doing them now.'
He began to walk slowly away from the table.
'Don't go Morgan. Let's talk about it.'
'I'm not going, I'm fetching another drink, this is going to be a five pint meeting at least.'
When Morgan got back with the drinks Matty had a look of resignation on his face.
'Ok,' he said, 'if you're not going to take my advice and snap their hands off over this Chazbatz opportunity there is something else that Peter in particular was very keen on. I have to stress to you Morgan, there is NO money in this at the moment. It's a development thing. They are developing a show that would be you, kind of travelling round cities of Britain looking at the crazy things that happen in them. That's it, that's all they've got, apart from a title, Grey Britain.'
Morgan was sitting bolt upright with a look of wild excitement in his eyes that Matty had never seen before.
'Yes. I LOVE it.'
'It's development. No money. You sign to be involved in a pilot, for which you get NO money. BUT if it gets picked up by a TV channel, and they've been talking to the BBC, then you get a good contract.'
'Would I be writing?'
'You could write some of it, but they have some writers lined up.'
'Me. On camera taking the piss out of Britain?'
'Well, that's not how they pitched it exactly, but..'
'I love it, where do I sign.'
'You'd have to commit to put your time in and there is always the chance that it doesn't fly and ...'
'It's what I'm talking about Matty. It's the break, it's me in my element, not trying to be a kids entertainer, I want it.'
'Ok, ok. I'll call Upchuck. I think you're going to regret letting Chazbatz go though.'

Elizabeth looked up from her computer and saw that her boss wasn't getting ready to leave her seat. The whole thing about bosses was that they had to be treated like children. 'Don't forget your meeting.' she said off-handedly, as if she wasn't saying,
'You've forgotten your friggin meeting haven't you?' The blank look that she got from Laura told her that she'd have to be a bit more direct. 'You have a meeting in ten minutes with Mr Chase over in his office.'
Laura frowned and then remembered,
'Oh, yes. We don't know what it's about do we?'
'No. We don't.'
Laura hadn't spoken to Arthur Chase since the night of the meal so she was curious to hear what he had to say now. It could be anything. It could be a promotion, although there wasn't really a position to be promoted to. It could be a raise, based on her outstanding performance and new business acumen. It was probably simply a new project that he wanted advice on. Whatever it was, it was unusual for Mr Chase to take a meeting himself.
Laura gathered together a few papers and props, just to appear professional and then made her way over to the far side of the building where Arthur had his office. He didn't come in every day but on the odd days that he did he worked the longest hours. It struck Laura as mildly old fashioned that Chase's secretary sat outside his office and operated as a gatekeeper. There was no 'open-door' policy at Steel and Caskett, but given the exorbitant rates that his time was charged out at he probably couldn't afford to be casually interrupted to discuss last night's TV.
Adjusting to the world of marketing for the legal profession hadn't been easy for Laura, who had cut her teeth in the gung-ho, seat of your pants arena of working for a go-ahead software company. Unfortunately, the software companies that Laura had worked for had all spectacularly imploded one by one. The constant leaving-dos and need to prove herself all over again became wearing. It left her with a

desire for security and stability but such mundane things come at a price and the cost was a time trip back twenty years. She was used to the constant sales verses marketing wars, the sales makes money, marketing spends money jibes and the view that all there was to marketing was knocking out a few brochures. What she wasn't used to was the lofty assumption that all marketing, and sales for that matter was somehow dirty. Ironic really when you looked at what some of the lawyers were prepared to do on a daily basis. Dispensing pain on behalf of their clients was done without so much as a blink. Laura didn't like to get too close to any of it, she glossed over the latest boardroom blood-lettings and mergers, reasoning that what she didn't know couldn't incriminate her. So there had been a lot to take on board, a steep learning curve as they liked to call it, but she had coped admirably and was now reaping the rewards. And the staid nature of the long standing Steel and Caskett certainly did the trick of making her feel a lot more secure, if not a little bored.

Arthur Chase's secretary pointed her through to Mr Chase's room and she was greeted by the seated and smiling kindly old gentleman. Arthur had not gone the route of most balding men these days in having what was left of his locks shaved off. He kept his white strands slicked to the sides of his head in a celebration of the hair that he could still muster. He didn't stand, but gestured for her to sit in the seat opposite him.

'Hello,' she said sitting, 'I haven't seen you since the night of the wonderful meal (she managed not to say, 'my' meal) so I just wanted to say how lovely that was.'

He nodded, his smile still in place. 'It was lovely wasn't it? I'm glad you enjoyed it, Iris certainly enjoyed herself and meeting you.' Iris was of course Arthur's wife and Laura was grateful that he'd mentioned her because Laura had not remembered her name and was dreading having to talk her way round it.

'Anyway, to business,' said Arthur allowing the smile to fade away.

'Brochure,' he said, holding up one of the glossy gate-fold documents that had been produced a few months before. They had gone down very well with everyone, and even though they had been expensive to produce they had already been a hit with new clients. Arthur was probably going to ask her to print off another five hundred or so, and amongst the papers on her knee she already had the costs.

'Spelling mistake,' he said. 'Page seven. It was brought to my attention by young Thomas in corporate. No one noticed it, but of course that's your job.'

Laura was feeling very, very hot in the face as her mind whirled through what on earth could have been missed. She had paid for the text to be professionally proofread before it had gone to print and knowing how pedantic the lawyers could be had spent a lot of time going over every letter herself.

'What was it?' she asked, the panic obvious in her voice.

'Oh, I'm not sure now. Something American, and we are an English firm,' he answered tossing the offending brochure to one side. 'The point is in our position we can't afford to have spelling errors. What on earth does that say about us Laura? About this firm and its attention to detail?'

'I understand, but I'm surprised Arthur. Mr Chase. I checked every word myself and had it double checked by a third party.'

'Still, it slipped through. Thankfully Dalfin was on his toes to avert a disaster.'

'Disaster?'

'Yes, with the seminar coming up we can't send these out. We'll have to have them re-printed. At great expense.' There was nothing kindly or friendly about Arthur Chase's eyes anymore, they were as cold as a P45 on a front door mat. 'It can't be allowed to happen.' he added, 'Not for Steel and Caskett. I was never in favour of taking a more commercial route for this company but I was out-voted by the other Partners. I hope that doesn't prove to be our undoing.'

Laura wanted to shout out. She wanted to ask if he was still talking about a spelling mistake, an error that he couldn't even remember the details of. She wanted to shake his stupid little head between her hands and ask if the end of the world could be put down to a spelling error.

Arthur checked his watch.

'I have a client coming in,' he said, 'You will have to excuse us for now, but I will expect you to put right the things you have failed in as soon as you can.'

Back at her desk Laura dragged open her desk drawer and dug out a copy of the brochure with shaking hands. She opened it to page seven expecting to see a misspelled headline glaring at her as if for the first time. Nothing. She poured over the 500 or so words for about an hour without being able to see a mistake. She read the words forwards and then backwards.

'I can't see it,' she said at last.

'What?' Elizabeth had been subtly watching Laura ever since she had come back ashen faced from her meeting.

'A spelling error on page seven.'

'I'd be surprised if there is. The sample batch had an error on seven and we put that right.' Elizabeth remembered everything, she was the safety net and it was inconceivable that she would have let a mistake through.

'Sample batch? Of course. We only had about five of those didn't we?'

'Yes, but they had 'initialise' with a 'z' because the computer kept putting in the American spelling.'

'Did we send any over to corporate?'

'Yes. But when we got the corrections we sent over the new ones.'

That had to be it. Thomas had kept one of the samples and taken that in to old fuck-face Chase to get her on the shit-list. And it was too late now, she would never be able to plead her case. Even if she managed to get a meeting with the old goat, he wouldn't listen. He was notoriously stubborn once he'd made his mind up. A working life of arguing cases irrespective of the rights and wrongs of the situation had made him impervious to the feelings of others. The damage was done, the impression had been left that she was a slacker. And what could she do? It flashed through her mind to start a campaign of her own to besmirch Thomas Dalfin based on his sexual strangeness, but she had no real evidence, no pictures or tapes and perhaps it was too close to real and actual blackmail.

Laura marched over to corporate, brochure under her arm and into the office that Thomas shared with three others. He glanced up shocked at her entrance.

'I need to talk to you.'

'I'm afraid I'm rather busy at the moment Laura. Schedule a meeting with Julie and we might be able to take five minutes in a couple of weeks.'

'We can do it here and now at full volume in the office Thomas or we can go to a meeting room now.' She didn't wait for him to answer, still exuding an air of professional calm, as if there was a very important project that needed some urgent input she walked to one of the empty meeting rooms and went in. A few moments later Thomas came in and shut the door behind him. He was visibly angry.

'You can't do this. I do not know what this is about Laura, but I do not approve of you coming to my desk...'

'It's about the brochure Thomas. It's about a conversation that I've just had with Arthur Chase. He seems to think I dropped a bollock over the brochure, but I know, and I think you know that I didn't. The copy he was looking at was a sample as well you know.'

'I don't know what you are talking about Laura, you seem somewhat hysterical but...'

'I'm very calm Thomas.'

He sighed and shook his head.

'Well I suppose it's just as well that we had this talk Laura. Listen the legal world is not for everyone. It demands the utmost dedication and attention to detail. If it turns out that you would be happier going back to the exciting fields of software, or even, I don't know, show business perhaps, then no one would blame you. I can assure you that you'd get glowing references from us at the moment.'
'At the moment?'
'Well, before you made any more mistakes.'
'I haven't made any mistakes Thomas, except perhaps in trusting you.'
Laura could see exactly how this was shaping up. It was the nastiest thing she'd ever faced and she wasn't quite sure what her next move should be.
'Did you read your contract of employment Laura? I doubt it because it's only boring old lawyers who can be bothered to read contracts.'
He was right about that, she'd been so keen to start that she'd barely scanned it, they were all the same these employment contracts anyway, weren't they? 'Did you read the part that said internet access while at work is forbidden for personal use? It's for business use only?'
'I never use the internet.' She quickly thought about whether she'd done any shopping online from her desk but she was sure that she hadn't.
'Really? The IT department has provided me with a log file that shows both you and Elizabeth have spent quite a long time recently searching for comedy sites of all things. I'd be interested to hear how that was for business use? I think Arthur might be interested in that too.'
Inside Laura's head she was telling herself, 'don't cry, don't cry'. Anger was building so fast that she was afraid that it would escape as tears. It was time to retreat, regroup and cry in the toilet if needs be. She nodded and turned to leave.
'Thomas, can I suggest that if you have any more of those sample brochures that you take them and lock them in a box. Lock them in a dark box so they feel very, very

helpless. I think they'd like that. And I think Arthur might be quite interested to hear about that too. After all, reputation is everything in a place like this.'

It was an empty threat, the word of a disgruntled employee wouldn't count for anything with Arthur Chase, but it was worth the stab.

As she turned the door handle Thomas took a stab back, and he was the professional.

'Yes, Arthur might, but I'm sure Chicken would as well. Be interested that is, in the things you think you know.'

The offices of Zingtastic were bright and modern in a way that made Chicken feel old and dull. There were casually dressed young adults casually milling around, and most of them were smiling. People smiling at work always made Chicken frown. Perhaps it was the latest front for the Moonies, he mused, a trendy marketing company would make a good cover for a religious cult.

The only reason that he had been able to rescue this interview was because Laura was such good mates with Katy the owner and boss. Anyone else would not have been able to survive the incredibly unprofessional way in which he had handled the whole thing. Katy was doing Laura a favour, there could be no doubt about that. Chicken certainly wouldn't have interviewed Chicken if he had been ignored and stood-up via email by Chicken as much as Katy had. Since returning from the mini-tour things had not gone well on the work front. In his own humble opinion, as a graphic designer Chicken was one of the best, but as a business developer he had to be the very worst in the country. He put it down to the fact that he wasn't greedy enough, he was too eager to please at too cheap a price and of course he was unmotivated and lazy. All the old contacts *said* that didn't have any work for him and couldn't see when that situation would change. Dunc wasn't even returning his messages. Meanwhile his comedy contacts were equally silent, the avalanche of paying gigs that he had hoped for after word got out about his tour support of Morgan had not materialised and he had to wonder if that was because word really had got out. When things are going badly it's only a very short jump from disappointment to paranoia, with the stepping stone of bitterness in-between. Getting up on stage and playing the fool was beginning to feel very like a very foolish indulgence to Chicken especially as this month he'd had to ask Laura to cover his half of the mortgage. Fortunately Laura's job at the law firm was very secure and she actually seemed to enjoy it.

Chicken sat in reception flicking through the design magazines and journals. He saw a stunning photograph of what could have been a cheese grater until on closer inspection he realised it was a library in Stockholm. Architecture was fascinating, some people managed to turn wonderful design ideas into actual massive multi-million pound buildings while Chicken couldn't even make a living. It was a cross-roads, Chicken had some serious decisions to make, exactly the kind that he was so bad at making.

'Are you waiting to see Katy?' Chicken looked up to see the grinning personal assistant.

'Yes,' he said, standing, 'that's right.'

'Good, you must be...' She looked down at her pad, unsure if she was reading correctly, 'Chick..'

'I'm Steven. Steven Spring.'

On the way home he sat on a park bench to think about things a little. It had turned out to be much more of a job than he'd thought. It was in front of him, a door to respectability and some kind of financial stability but he'd have to step out of the corridor of uncertainty and comedy. The interview had gone very well and not only because the boss was a friend of Laura's. In fact she had made that very clear right at the start, she wasn't about to carry anyone in her business. She needed a manager, someone to keep the twenty somethings in-line and productive but not stifle their creativity. A studio manager who was a little more mature than the flighty

graduates that filled the design studio, but who could still 'walk the walk'. As much as he hated that phrase he'd smiled and nodded, already talking on some corporate style.
As she talked he found himself thinking that he certainly could do the job, he might even like it, but he'd have to commit, he'd have to put in the hours get in early and concentrate. He'd have to take it seriously if it was going to work out. In short he'd have to give up the late nights of gigging.
He leaned back on the bench and watched the people go past, his fellow commuters. Join us, they seemed to be saying in their steady trudging. He didn't know why he had fallen out of love with stand-up on the trip with Morgan, but that's what had happened. He'd seen it for what it was, he'd awoken to the reality of the game. But still, was he really ready to give it up?

When Chicken finally arrived home Laura was sitting on the sofa in the kitchen, quiet and still and he saw instantly she'd been crying. His first thought was that she must have heard from her mate Katy and that he hadn't got the job. He was hit by a wave of deep disappointment. It surprised him how much he suddenly wanted that job. He'd already started visualising his new life.
'What's up darling?' he asked slumping down next to her.
Laura told him it all, well, all of it that he needed to know. She'd had a bad day at work, the management were ganging up on her and they were finding fault with her work.
'Right. Well my interview went well.'
She brightened, having forgotten that that was where he'd been. 'Really? That's great. You saw Katy?'
'Well she is the boss, and this is a management role.'
Her mental computer was already plotting outcomes.'
If Chicken could get the job at Zingtastic, then it would give her the chance to leave Steel and Caskett and start up as a Freelance Marketing Consultant. It was something that she'd always wanted to try, but had never dared with Chicken's

student earning power. It was good news and if he actually started to earn some money she could push ahead with the other plans, the extension and the other thing, the thing she hadn't told him about yet.
'Brilliant, brilliant. Did she say when she'd let you know?'
'Not really, she said that she had a couple of other people to see.'
'Did you get on with her?'
'Yes.'
'No stupid jokes?'
'No. I was Steven.'
She hugged him and the kiss she gave him still tasted of the tears that had been forced out by Thomas and Arthur.

It was late and it was dark and only those that took their jobs very seriously were still at their desks. Thomas walked into Arthur's office and sat in the same chair that Laura had been in earlier.
'Thanks for taking a few minutes Arthur. I just wanted to say that I see no problems, but sometimes when a subordinate has been reprimanded, it can cause some bad feeling. I wanted to say that if any accusations or rumours or slurs surface I shall be forced to deal with them most robustly.'
Arthur took off his glasses and put them to one side.
'Thomas, you are very valuable to this firm. I look after things of value.' He picked up his glasses as if the conversation was over. Thomas stood.
'Do you know what her husband does by the way? He's an unknown comedian.'
'Comedian? Good God. She never mentioned that before. Might be worth getting her CV out and having a look. Compare it to some research. Might be some other things that she isn't telling us.' As Thomas began to leave Arthur said, 'And Thomas, I know it's been hard on you, the divorce and everything and some of your ex-wife's outlandish statements, but I would advise that you keep all personal life well away from the office in future.'

'Oh, don't worry Arthur. I certainly will.'

His soul boosted by the knowledge that he'd soon be on TV Morgan did a great show. Three nights a week he appeared at a comedy chain called Jollysters. It was a regular well paid stint although much maligned by the comedians that couldn't get gigs there. It was true that it tended to be the Hen and Stag party crowd or office loud-mouths with their ties hilariously tied around their foreheads, but it was work. The food was the usual freezer to fryer pub variety and the pissed up punters sat at long wooden tables waiting to be insulted. The bonus for the comedians was that there were bouncers at the back and any especially obnoxious cretins were efficiently removed. The other fact that was resented by comedians was that Jollysters and their venues in major cities held the key to whether a working comedian could make a living. Three nights a week and then other gigs on top meant that you could do it as a job, IF you weren't a well known TV face. The bitter ones were the comedians who for a variety of reasons, such as not turning up, turning up late or doing way too long instead of their assigned 30 minutes could be black-listed and suddenly see their income plummet.
As much as he liked the regular money Morgan was looking forward to leaving it all behind. TV faces didn't play Jollysters because you had to change your act. Jollysters forced the crowd to consume comedy in a certain way and if you were going to retain your spot you had to keep to the programme. It got kind of boring in truth. But still, tonight with the pilot for Grey Britain only weeks away Morgan could afford to see Jollysters in a new rosy light. God it was good to be a comedian. He didn't have to get up early and he didn't need to fill in forms, he just needed to be funny, night after night after night. And could he, good old bullet-proof Morgan do it? Of course he could, it was as easy as falling off a greased up high-class prostitute.

NINE

God, how time flies when you are having F. U. N. It had been a crazy, mad, mental, two years, thankfully in a frenetic unpredictable way, rather than bi-polar or schizophrenic fashion. In short things had changed a lot in a short time span.
He still couldn't get used to the feeling that he got on nights like this, and every night was like this now. There were perhaps six hundred people out there in the auditorium and they had come to see him. His face was on the huge posters hanging outside that allowed his image to stare wistfully down at the tourists of the West End. Some of the passersby even pointed up and laughed at his pictures when they saw them, he was *that* funny. His name was on the tickets that they had purchased well in advance meaning that this show had been sold out for weeks. Since his regular TV appearances had begun that happened every night now. He was a draw, he was hot and he was absolutely loving it. And the bonus was that the more he loved it the funnier he seemed to get. It wasn't quite Wembley Arena yet but according to Peter, his ever smiling manager, that wasn't too far off. It was for the taking if he wanted it.
Unlike so many who broke through from student gigs he had cross audience appeal, from grannies to kids and all the trendy middle ground too. He hadn't lost the students on the journey, not all of them anyway, they were still turning up. It had been a very fast rise and people weren't sick of him yet so he was trying to squeeze as much as he could out of everything while life was good. He was saying yes to everything with no cares for over-exposure. He agreed readily to any interview, no matter how buried on the internet it was going to be. He had merchandise deals and adverts lined up and if he could get a breakfast cereal named after him he was going to go for that too. Initially his manager had tried to counsel him to keep some of his powder dry, but dry

powder wasn't in his nature and he was aware that if the window of opportunity should shut it would be very hard to push it open again. Some liked to play the mystery card, to keep them guessing and wanting more, but his approach was to give them everything now and hope they came back for another dose. His tactic was to drag as much through the open window as possible and try to jam it open that way. He stood at the wings and watched the warm up act, a comedy magician, chosen for the fact that he wasn't very good, not good enough to steal the show anyway. In the front row he could make out the circles of faces, waiting, anticipating his arrival on stage. He was excited with not a trace of nerves. He knew it was going to be the best night since the night before. His material just flowed at the moment. In an evening he was doing maybe an hour and a bit , 50 percent of which was improvised there and then. Brand new, topical comedy fresh every night. He was **THAT** funny. Who would have believed that he, Danny, no more than an office drone could manage the climb?

Imagine, it had all started at that fateful gig in Scarborough only two years before. He shook his head at the memory. He'd been ready to crawl away. He'd been ready to leave comedy alone for ever and concentrate on his normal job; to join the ranks of the poor souls trudging through daily hell towards their non-existent pensions and eventual anonymous graves. Who could have imagined that the destructive and humiliating act of being an abusive heckler had turned his life around? For him a kind of therapy and it hadn't cost him anything either, he hadn't even bought his own ticket.

His sister had been correct in her amateur psychoanalysis, his unhinged behaviour that night was just a sign of how badly he wanted it. She had forgiven him for the fact that they didn't see the friends anymore that had come with them to the club that night. Her husband Brian had let it go too, but he'd had a quiet word with Danny to ask that he didn't use inappropriate language in front of the kids. As if he was about to start heckling the children for not doing their homework?

Danny had written his plan down in the meeting room at work and then followed it through to the letter, never deviating or faltering. With a certain amount of dumb luck that he liked to think of as talent he was now reaping the benefits. The main thing was the change in him. After the Scarborough incident, he had experienced a strange lifting of pressure. He saw clearly that it didn't matter, none of it mattered, it was just talking and if he wanted to stand on a stage and spout he really didn't care whether people listened, let alone laughed. He no longer had any plans to be a rich and famous comedian, he only wanted to spend his time doing it. He had some things he wanted to say, and he found them funny which was enough.

From the first gig he just knew things were going to work, because he absolutely didn't care whether they did or not. It was some kind of inexplicable cosmic reverse psychology, he wasn't trying but it started to happen. His devil may care attitude allowed him to tap into a rich reservoir of comic truth, it was something that hit home with audiences everywhere. It also helped that in only Danny's second gig not one but two entertainment journalists happened to be there, they also happened to off their faces and in love and they both remembered and reported a much better gig than he had done. Even he couldn't understand the lopsided coverage he got from the Drowning Parrot pub. The headliner never got a mention, nor did any of the other comedians, but he alone got a rave review. He read it and shrugged. It wasn't justified but he simply thought, so be it. Like football, sometimes you don't get a penalty that you should have had and other times you get awarded one that never should have been. He was going to take his kick and slot it in the top corner.

Newspapers make opinion and soon word started to spread and bookings got easier to find. He entered rowdy gong shows and won them. He dealt with hecklers with the utter contempt that they deserved but in truth there weren't very

many. He was such an energetic force on stage that hecklers didn't really get a chance to get a word in.
It began to be a bit of a blur with gigs every other night, then every night. All the time his confidence was growing and his act was going from strength to strength. He lucked out when a big newcomer competition turned up, some of the acts dropped out and he happened to have a free night. Amongst a reduced and largely awful group of no-hopers he won the competition, not even realising what the prize was. It turned out that the winner had the chance to appear on a local radio station. He turned up, kept it clean and talked like he was born to be on radio. The station invited him back when the phone response to his slot went wild with members of the public ringing in to ask where they could see him live. Peter, who wasn't his manager at the time, was on his way to a meeting in the car, he heard the show and spotted an opportunity to replace his recently deceased cash cow.
The first thing his new manager did was some pruning of Danny's schedule, he cut out the gigs that weren't going to take him anywhere and added in plenty that were. He upped Danny's appearance fee and after only a year Danny Childs was able to chuck in his day job. The morning he walked into that office, past Jonathan and some of the others who had seen his first ever awful gig to hand in his resignation was a moment of pure joy. Touchingly they either weren't jealous or they hid it well and gave him the thumbs up, back slaps and a rousing cheer as he left the building. Somehow he had done it. He was making a living out of doing a thing that he enjoyed. It really was living the dream and at that stage, a year ago, it was enough. That was before his manager worked on his ambition, before he realised how much it could grow, how far it could go, before he started to want the world.

The warm-up finished and the crowd began to bubble with restless anticipation, the waiting was over and it was time for him to hit that stage. The noise engulfed him like the most

comfortable duvet he'd ever had. For the first minute of stage time he drank some water and waited for the cheering and clapping to die down. Eventually he took the mike, shaded his eyes and said,
'Blimey, you managed to get here then.' It wasn't a joke, it wasn't in itself funny but the laughter rolled over him. He was that funny now, his reputation made it funny. He could say anything and they would laugh, because they believed as much as he did that right now he was as funny as it was possible to be. It was going to be another wonderful night.

Davis looked at his piled high desk and his overfilled to-do list and shook his head. What had it come to? He couldn't believe that he even had a to-do list. The one thing that he had never wanted from life was a proper job, in fact it had been his mission to avoid getting sucked in, and yet here he was fully sucked. Running four busy clubs for the Grand Hotel chain in the North East of England was as proper a job as he was ever likely to get. And Ray was his boss. That was the other thing he hated, he had a boss. He didn't like saying that at all, 'my boss this' or 'my boss that.' It stuck in his throat, so most of the time if he absolutely had to mention it he'd say, 'the guy I'm working with' or 'my business partner'. But in reality, Ray was his boss and acted like he was. Davis had targets, he had KPIs and he had regular catch-up, strategy and planning meetings. He might as well be working for a bank. Or a multi-national fast-food corporation at least, which was a better analogy because that was the way they served up the fun to the East Coast punters.
The initial attractions of being the big chief of entertainment in the wild winds of the North had been seductive. It gave Davis a regular, if not huge, income and more than that status. The comedians who merely used to kiss his arse for gigs now wanted to devour it. He had control of the bookings for four gigs one after another which was a week's work as far as a comedian was concerned. And to get the good guys

to come up north he was paying decent money. A lot of old 'friends' had come out of the woodwork in the couple of years that he'd been building the reputation of the clubs. He'd become popular. All of that was good, what was not so good was the way the clubs had developed and the amount of boring admin type work he'd had to take on. He had imagined himself swanning into full and vibrant venues when the night was kicking off and ready to go but it just didn't happen like that. Instead he was on the phone constantly filling in for no-show comedians and organising the paraphernalia of promotion. The website, the facebook pages and twitter posts, the posters, the newspaper listings, the tickets and on and on. The organisation of fun was not fun in itself and what had been an amusing distraction with one club to run had frankly become a chore.

He'd talked to Ray about hiring someone else to do the donkey work, after all they were at the seaside, but he wasn't prepared to fund another body, especially as Davis was doing so well, even if he was a bit too negative these days. Ray feared that if he let him relax a little the momentum would be lost and he didn't want to lose that just yet. Ray always had plans. The one thing that gave Davis a tiny spark of pride was that he had made himself indispensible and it was a cushioned status that he'd never enjoyed before. The clubs couldn't run without him and Ray would be like a duck not only out of water but drowning in hot soup without him.

So Davis carried on but it was like a golden jail. He now had so much more to lose than when it had only been the one night a week. The frustrating thing was that Ray knew it and was using it to his own advantage.

The other thing that aggravated Davis much more than he thought it would was the slide towards the middle of the road comedians that he had embraced. He'd been hasty in agreeing to aim at the older audience. He wanted the edgy and dangerous performers but Ray insisted on broad appeal comedy hacks. Davis liked to book up-and-coming talent because they were cheaper and more grateful but Ray wanted tried and tested crowd pleasers. Davis thought that over time he'd be able to live with this move to the mainstream that he'd learn to treat comedy as comedy and enjoy it all no matter what. He was wrong. He felt as though he had sold his soul and the scary apparition of ending up as entertainment officer on a cruise ship haunted him nightly. Here he was, a man who had stood on stage at the Hackney Empire in a pair of Y-fronts, now reduced to promoting comedy plate spinners in a hotel in Bridlington.

He pushed aside the to-dos and turned to his one true friend, the internet. Even though he was out in the sticks he tried to keep up with what was happening in the real world and subscribed to a number of email newsletters and forums. Following a link he read a review about some new kid called Danny. Fighting down the envy he skimmed it. The kid was hot, yadda, yadda. There was a small interview with him, Davis was scanning it when his eye was grabbed and held. He read again. 'Blah, blah, blah, ...it all started for me at some crummy club on a horrible Saturday night in Scarborough a couple of years ago. I owe it all to that night.' Davis sat up. That had to mean his club. Had to, he was the only one running a Saturday night comedy club in Scarborough back then. He owed it all to the club in Scarborough. Oh man, those were the days. Davis did some searching and found some publicity shots of the kid. He scrutinised the little jpegs and frowned. He couldn't say that he remembered him, but he must have booked him at some point otherwise how could he have started in Scarborough? He began printing some of the stuff off to use it for publicity, 'You saw him here first' 'we bring you the stars of tomorrow' that kind of thing and then enthusing for the first time in ages he thought that he should put a call into the guy's agent. Maybe he'd be prepared to come back up to 'boro for old time's sake? Even though according to all the online press he was massive at the moment and not short of a gig or two, comedians were a sentimental bunch and if

Davis could get him to come up to revisit the place where it had all started for him it would be quite a coup. But it was more than that. There was of course a selfish element for Davis, there always was. It might be a rebirth for him. If he could convince Ray that comedy needed its raw excitement maybe they could make at least one of the clubs worth going to? Maybe he could recapture some of the old spirit of groundbreaking comedy. Maybe he could get back to not doing a job.

Chicken surveyed the office, his little empire, but he wasn't Chicken anymore, he was Steven. Long ago Steven Spring at the hands of cruel classmates had mutated into Spring Chicken, then Chicken and like all hated nicknames it stuck. Eventually, when he started doing stand-up comedy he liked it, but it had taken a real job to unravel the name to its former glory. He was now a serious and respected design studio manager. It hadn't been as easy as he'd thought it would be to bury his comedy past, the reverberations had echoed across the internet for quite a while, cached and stored to pop up when he least expected it. Some of the listings he'd actively unsubscribed from like the UK Comedian's Database, which fortunately took down his entry and embarrassing publicity picture pretty much when he'd asked them to. Other widely accessible digital evidence he had no control over and simply had to wait until new gigs and new comedians moved him down the charts. A useful thing was that he had never been much of a fan of the numerous comedy forums and internet chat rooms that were haunted by teenaged virtual comedians who could talk a good gig but probably rarely set foot on a stage. In fact he hated that whole cyber-world of bedroom experts so he'd never bothered much with it, meaning that there was no foot-print to remove. He was also helped in his quest for anonymity by the fact that there was nothing out there under his real name, which was another reason that he insisted on being Steven at work.

Part of his new role was meeting and liaising with clients, and some of them were very respectable and conservative businesses, so it had been part of Katy's request (request NOT order) that he play down his comedy hobby. She knew about it through Laura of course, and while she didn't mind herself, she could see that it might be an issue for the likes of Crandish Bank. In truth he'd been more than willing to oblige. He wanted a break from it. He wanted to be taken seriously and as time went on the need to maintain his steady income had multiplied. He needed to be respected by his staff, the six young designers who worked under him, and so he told none of them and none of them knew that he'd once considered himself a comedian.

Chicken did receive an invitation from James, the man who ran the gig in Hull, his last good one. It was on a Thursday, asking if he could make it to Hull by the next night to do a 15 minute spot to replace another comedian who had dropped out. For ten minutes Steven's Chicken persona had been excited, but it was silly, simply the buzz of being asked. He didn't have a chance of driving up to Hull not just because the unfixable Mitsubishi had been scrapped but mainly because he just didn't feel like a comedian anymore. The emails for gigs petered out after a few months and it proved to Steven that unless he'd been prepared to put an enormous amount of energy into keeping the ball rolling, it was going to stop and be covered in moss in no time. He felt a slight regret about that but he suppressed it very well. He forced himself not to think about the contrasts he had adjusted to. However, there were still the tough days, and today was turning out to be one. Adam, one of his staff had been to a comedy club the night before and everyone wanted to hear about it apart from Steven who kept silent while pretending to work. Behind him Adam said,
'And the first guy came on, he was rubbish, it was embarrassing. And then another bloke, he was alright, and then the headline bloke, he was brilliant. He came out with some excellent stuff.' Of course Adam couldn't remember all

of the comedians but he did remember the main comedian's name. 'Morgan, he was called, really slick. Professional. My girlfriend said that she was sure she'd seen him in a commercial once but she couldn't remember what it was.'
'Yoghurt.' Steven muttered under his breath.
Adam was loud and he was being quizzed by his interested colleagues, who saw an opportunity to do anything but work for a few minutes. Steven had no choice but to grit his teeth and listen.
'He was talking about, you know when you go through the airport security. Soo funny. I was pissing myself.'
Steven heard it all, in fact he'd heard it all before first hand. It sounded like Morgan was doing the same act that he'd been doing for six years. Since their trip up north (God, had he really done that?) despite himself Steven had kept his eye on the TV wondering if anything had ever come of the York gig and the much awaited TV execs. He'd never seen Morgan in anything, but he could have missed it.
'Oh right, yeah, he did this joke right about someone calling him a tight twat,' Steven closed his eyes as the profanity unfolded. He shook his head, so Morgan had stolen one of his best jokes. Well, he guessed he wasn't using it now. It was a compliment really, if you thought about it. Nice even that Morgan was indirectly making money out of something that Steven, or more accurately Chicken had thought up. Chicken's intellectual property out making its own way in the world.
The office discussion turned to comedy clubs in general and whether they were a good thing. Most of his staff were young enough to still appreciate them. And then they started talking about comedians that they'd seen on TV. Danny Childs was a name that cropped up, but it wasn't anyone that Steven had ever heard of. When he could take no more he lifted his head, as if he'd heard nothing of the chat.
'Adam?'
'Yes?'
'How's the holiday magazine spread coming on?'

'Oh, pretty good.'
'Ok, don't forget, deadline's Friday.'
'Yes, I'm on it boss. Just need to re-touch that image of a caravan.'
Adam came over to his desk.
'So, you got a favourite comedian Steve?' he asked.
'Um, not much makes me laugh these days Adam. Must be my age.'
Adam did not contradict him, he seemed perfectly prepared to accept that a person of Steven's decrepit 36 years was past having fun.
'You should come out some time with us. We go to the Digging Dog on Albermarle street. It's only £6 to get in.'
On the tip of Steven's tongue was 'I used to play that club. I've been on that stage.' but all he said was,
'Right. Sounds good.' In a way that Adam could understand meant that he wasn't ever going to join them.

Steven waited until everyone was gone that night before he accessed his pass-worded 'Comedy' folder on his Apple. He opened the file 'Design Game' and began to write. After about an hour he saw Katy coming out of her office to go home and quickly closed the document. As she passed Katy said,
'Always working late Steve. You aren't impressing me. I don't want your misses saying that I'm overworking you and stopping you from getting home. Especially now.'
'I know, just had a couple of things that I needed to finish and I won't get a chance to do them when I get home.'
It was true, he'd never be able to concentrate at home and although he felt quite guilty at not hurrying back, it was for a greater cause. 'Design Game' was his lottery ticket, and it was the only thing keeping him sane.

Even though it was still only seven o'clock Steven let himself in quietly just in case the baby was asleep, but she wasn't,

and he was pleased to see she was sitting on Laura's knee having a story read to her.
'Look Heather, it's daddy.' His year-old daughter smiled and giggled as he put down his laptop and reached over to pick her up. After leaning over and kissing his wife he did the daddy things for Heather, the cooing and baby talk, the cuddling and lifting up high.
'You were a bit late tonight.'
'Yes, sorry, had to finish something.'
'Anyway, I kept her up to see you. Do you want to put her to bed while I go and have a bath?'
'Yes, I'd love to.' answered Steven, and he meant it too.
He bounced Heather on his knee. He hadn't told either of his girls that he'd been working on their future. It was more than a lottery ticket. Ever since he'd given up on live comedy Chicken was buried but he had been bubbling with ideas that went nowhere, until he started to spend his lunch times working on a sit-com script. He'd written and re-written the 40 odd pages of snappy dialogue until he was pleased with it and now he was nearly ready to take it to the next level.
Steve's plan was to track down Kevin, the writer that they had stayed with when he and Morgan had been in York on Steve's last tour. Kevin was a sit-com writer, so he had to have contacts and at the very least he would be able to tell Steve who he could send his script to. He'd watched a fair amount of network TV and he was convinced that what he'd committed to paper was better than most of the shows that were broadcast.
Steve whispered in Heather's ear so Laura couldn't overhear him even though he knew she was in the bathroom upstairs. He wasn't embarrassed or ashamed of what he was doing, he simply wanted it to be the best surprise ever.
'Daddy's going to get something on telly Heather. Then Daddy can work from home like Mummy does. Then we can all be at home. Won't that be fun? Heather giggled and he kissed the top of her head. 'God, that would be brilliant.' He said.

TEN

'What I want to do,' said Davis 'is see if we can get some new breaking talent to come up, like this guy Danny Childs. I know, I know, he's too big for us but I read that he started his career in my club so I figure he owes me. I asked around the internet and it turns out that I know a bloke who used to have the same agent so I think I can get a call in. He'll be glad to revisit the old haunts I'm sure. He's going to be huge and it would put us on the map. People see him on TV and know that we broke him, it has to be good for us. He..'
'Forget it.' Ray was behind his desk sorting through staff schedules and only paying Davis a small amount of attention. He'd been distracted and offhand from the moment Davis had come in even though it was him who'd called the meeting. He was frowning a lot too.
'What?'
'I'm not interested in new and fresh we've been through this a thousand times Davis, I want tried and tested. I want material that the punters recognise.'
'Well, they will, this guy's all over the TV at the moment.' Ray wrinkled his nose.
'I know. I've seen him on a couple of things on the television. I know my comedy Davis, and I'm not keen.'
'Not keen? He's fucking dynamite at the moment. He's filling clubs in the West End'
'Too smutty.'
'Smutty? He's funny.' Davis hadn't actually heard Danny's act but he was taking it as read that he would be funny. Ray pushed his papers to one side.
'Look Davis this meeting is more about you really. About you and me. What I need is someone who is in tune with me. A person who can just put on the shows that I want. I have the plans, I have the ideas, I just want someone to follow through. I don't want input, I want output.'

'Ray, I DO know comedy. This is what I do. You have to give the crowds something new or they stop coming in.'
Ray sighed.
'In a way I think you are right Davis and that's why I am going to give them something new. A new entertainments manager in fact.'
At last, thought Davis, a new grunt to do the boring admin for him.
'I've got an old mate who's been booking for one of the cruise lines. He's going to give it a go for a season and we'll see how it pans out. Thank you, for everything.'
'Wait a minute. Give what a go?'
'Your job.'
'What about me?'
'You're out.'
'OK, we'll forget Danny Childs.'
'It's not about any one comedian Davis, it's the whole thing. I just don't feel like you have your heart in it anymore. I get the feeling that all the admin is getting you down.'
'Bullshit. I live for admin.'
'I get the feeling that the type of audience we play to isn't your cup of tea.'
'Crap. Punters are punters and comedy is comedy. Come on Ray, we're partners. Sort of. I do the comedy and you do...' he gestured around wildly, 'the place.'
'I feel that you don't necessarily have the best interests of this hotel chain uppermost in your mind.'
'But you can't take my clubs. I made them. They are me.'
'No Davis, they are part of the Grand Hotel chain, and no one's bigger than the Grand chain. Not even you.'
'I'll sue you.' Ray didn't even smile evilly at that.
'Nothing was ever signed by either of us Davis. You can't sue, all you can do is go away and cry. So, jog on.'

Peter laid it out very simply for an exhausted Danny Childs. There were things that he wanted Danny to understand and he didn't want him to give an impulsive knee jerk reaction that might not be in everyone's best interests. Danny had not long come off stage and he was now sitting on a battered old sofa in his empty dressing room. It was a sign of how far he'd come that he actually had a dressing room these days. He was still buzzing with after show glow, the adrenaline and adoration still spicing up his blood. Soon he would crash a little so knowing this Peter wanted to ride the vibe while everything still looked rosy.

He patted Danny on the knee paternally.

'Great show. One of your best Danny my boy.'

'Thanks. It did go well didn't it? Dipped a bit in the middle maybe?' Peter smiled to himself. Always the self-doubt, always the fishing for compliments, never really certain, no wonder so many artists ended up as basketcases.

'Nonsense. They were eating out of the palm of your hand.'

'Yes, pretty much.'

'They wouldn't let you come off.' It was true Danny had taken a number of encores.

'Got to capitalise on that kind of talent my friend. Which brings me to the business end of the show.' He took some papers from his briefcase. 'You have a choice Danny, and it's your choice alone. I can advise, but it's your career and I wouldn't presume to stick my oar in *unless* you asked me to.' He held up his empty hand to show exactly how hands-off he was. 'My role is to present the opportunities, you are the artist, the talent and it's you who has to deliver, so I'm not going to push.'

'Push what?' Danny was the onstage talent, he knew it, but he also knew that without Peter he would probably still be scarping away in the office to fund his comedy. It wasn't that he was exactly grateful to Peter, Peter was doing well enough out of the set-up, it was that he could see the need for Peter. At the moment anyway.

'The choice is as I mentioned before. The studio in America has come up with an offer of a cameo part for you in the next Ben Stiller movie.' Danny's luck had been holding out, a producer on a stay-over in London had caught some of

Danny's act on T.V. He was always looking for that one special piece of the creative jigsaw that would lift a movie. It struck a note with him that there might be a slot for a hot new British talent in the film he was putting together. If they couldn't get Gervais anyway.

'They wanted to see some of your tapes, I sent them over and they liked what they saw. It's Hollywood and it's an absolute cracker. Good money but it's a small part. Who knows, could end up on the cutting room floor, but I don't need to tell a clever boy like you what it could lead to, sky's the limit. You might get noticed big time but it has to be said, fuck it up and you won't get another chance. It's a tough market and in general they don't like Brits. Gervais, sure he's done alright, but plenty, plenty of English comedy bones lying in those Hollywood graveyards.'

'And the choice?'

'Meanwhile, at exactly the same time the good old BBC have jumped off the fence, got their fingers out of their arses and signed some forms.'

'You're painting a picture Peter, and I'm feeling sick.'

'They want you for the new sit-com that we talked about. Some shit about a comedy detective. For you it's the way into the mainstream TV landscape. Not just one off appearances like you've been doing, but a whole sit-com based on you. You will be very much the star.'

'Ok.' Nothing good could surprise Danny these days, more and more it was as if it was all due to him and he was simply mopping it up. He was getting what he deserved and it was ALL good.

'The thing is Dan, you have to choose one or the other. The shooting schedules clash, well they overlap, so that's where your choice comes in.'

'So, I have to choose Hollywood chance or BBC job?'

'Yes.'

'Both. I choose both.'

'I thought you might say that Danny and I like your ambition.' In fact Peter had been banking on it.

'OK, leave it with me, this is what we do, we can't make the film studio wait, because to them at the moment you're pretty much nothing, but we can string the BBC along, we'll commit and promise and then delay. It's a risk, but only a slight one. Knowing them they'll end up delaying anyway.'
'Let's play the game. Let's be players.'
'Ok, I'll get on it. Phone calls to make.' He stood up, and then paused like Columbo, 'Oh, one other thing. How do you feel about guesting at a couple of L.A. gigs while you're over there? Just a couple to kind of get a feel of the states? Test the water sort of thing?'
'Why not, since we're going to be there anyway.'
'Brilliant. Right, now don't forget to get some rest Danny, you've got an early call tomorrow for the voice over stuff over in soho.'
'Right. The comedy lemon in the insurance ad.'
'It's money for old rope, you'll be done by one o'clock. In and out, bish, bash, bosh.'
'Smash and grab.'
'And then you've got the kids comedy awards to present on kids zone T.V. in the afternoon. So mind your language.'
'Why am I doing that exactly? I mean it's not really my thing, kids T.V.?'
'No, no, I told you, you're not in it, you're the honoured guest. It sets a tone, it puts you up there. Besides, they're the fans of tomorrow. Who do you think accesses all the comedy downloads these days?'

Steven was incredibly nervous his finger over the buttons of his phone. It reminded him of those minutes when he used to be waiting to go on and just how uncomfortable it could be. It had taken him a day to track down the number and now he was almost too scared to use it. He braced himself and dialled.
'Hello? Is that Kevin?'
'Yup.'

'Hi, you might not remember me, I stayed at your house a couple of years ago with Morgan? I was a comedian?'
'Was?'
'Yeah, well anyway, do you remember?'
'Yup. You took off early.'
In the background Steven could hear a typewriter. 'Is your name Turkey?'
'It was Chicken, now it's Steven. Steven Spring.'
'Hardly, Bond, James Bond is it? But Spring Chicken, I like that.'
'So, how's it going with you Kevin?'
'I'm over 40 and so is my waistband, what can I tell you?'
'Right. Listen Kev, the thing is I've been writing.' he heard the typewriter stop. 'it's a sit-com, I've called it Design Game. I was wondering...'

Her self-employed marketing consultancy career had hardly got going before Laura fell pregnant with Heather. It was probably bad planning and certainly bad timing, but how many of the truly important things in life could be planned? The break from Steel and Caskett had been as cold as the ice in their hearts and the steel in their name. She thought perhaps that there would be a little gratitude shown that she was removing herself from a situation that had become uncomfortable for everyone, but she should have known better than to expect favours from lawyers. Perhaps it was something to do with them not being seen to admit liability but very little was said to her officially. To save a little face she resigned in a bluster of, 'I'm setting up my own business as a consultant.', 'The time is right.' and 'It's something that I've always wanted to do.'.
Laura hadn't confided the growing corporate nastiness to Elizabeth and so apparently not knowing all the details her P.A. had reacted as if very shocked. But there was something about Elizabeth's surprise, a certain wrong note, that made Laura wonder if she actually knew more than she was saying.

The next day she saw Thomas in the corridor and he nodded stony faced.
'Sorry to hear that you are leaving,' he said, 'I just wanted you to know that we are thinking of promoting Elizabeth into your position. As I understand it she's been covering most of the detail anyway.'
She could have said, 'Fuck off.' or 'You shit bag.' But she didn't, she acted as if untouched by the mortifying, belittling dig and said nothing.
She went home and in a rage threw the cook book that featured Jago Steller's smarmy face away. She didn't want to be reminded of that evening in his restaurant when for a few moments she had allowed herself to be hypnotised by reflected fame and glamour.
Laura's only regret was that she hadn't been able to hang on long enough to take maternity leave with Steel and Caskett, but of course the pregnancy hadn't been on the calendar. It was on the life road-map and the horizon but not in the diary. So, for the first few months, between hospital visits and antenatal classes she concentrated on her new role and rang round business contacts and sent a ton of emails. Slowly she began to acquire clients and then very suddenly she was as busy as she could possibly manage.
The biggest surprise, more so than the growing baby in her womb, was Chicken's transformation into Steven. The morphing was well under way once he was hired by Zingtastic, (Katy took a chance for Laura's sake), but the change really took hold once he knew he was going to be a father. There was no other way to describe it than to say he 'knuckled down'. He sometimes worked late, and he stopped going out to comedy gigs as he was tired most evenings by the time he came home. He had responsibilities and he was acting responsibly. He even stopped talking about comedy or referring to himself as a comedian. He was a Design Studio Manager now. And then Heather stopped threatening to join them and actually burst into their lives, and since then there hadn't really been time to blink. But there were times,

lost minutes of sleeping baby silence when Laura found herself wondering if Chicken had become just a little bit duller and greyer as Steven Spring. He'd been carrying the nickname of Chicken since school and was saddled with it when she met him, so there was something odd about him jettisoning it so late in his life. But still, if it was what he wanted it was fine with her.

Davis was standing in the quiet chip shop just before the lunchtime rush talking to the spotty young bloke who was standing behind the painfully shiny steel counter that threw back his blotched reflection. It couldn't help but cross Davis's mind that the kid was like an inverse advert. Eat chips and get spotty. It was like the really fat lass that worked in Burger King in the high street.
'So as I said I used to run those four clubs, the ones in the hotels, all of them, I was in charge of the whole operation but in the end it wasn't for me. You know why? I'll tell you why, it was all about squeezing money from punters with them, money, money, money from old-aged pensioners and I'm about the comedy. I'm about funny, funny, funny. I used to be a comedian, won a few competitions and now I'm about finding new talent and getting it out there, I live for the comedy. Have you heard of Danny Childs? He's been on telly, I discovered him, right there in Scarborough, he played my club and he's never looked back and if you don't believe me look it up on the internet. Google it, Danny Childs, Scarborough. It'll come up. He started with me and so have loads of others. Loads. So I've got a new club now. Do you know the old Railway Tavern? Been done up. I'm upstairs on Wednesday nights with this new comedy club I'm calling it, 'Giving a rat's arse'. Good headliners and new comedians. You should come down.'
'Right, anyway, do you want any chips?'
'I'll tell you what I'll do, I'll buy some chips if you put this poster up.'
'It's not really up to me.'

'So where's the manager?'

'He lives in Spain.'

'He's not going to know then is he? I'll put it up now and you can give me a portion of chips.'

Davis was back to what he knew best, booking the acts that made him feel like he was at the cutting edge and utilising guerrilla, seat of the pants promotion. His earnings had taken quite a hit after he'd left the Grand and he was now back in debt but his emotional bank was full. He thought of it as 'left' rather than sacked because his innate pride and self image couldn't cope with the thought that a know-nothing twat like Ray could sack him. He had rationalised it by convincing himself that he had been unhappy and on the cusp of quitting and it hadn't taken long for him to completely accept that story and change it in his mind to the scenario that he'd actually gone to that meeting with Ray to chuck it all in. Once he'd retold the tale to a couple of interested friends he had rewritten history into the classic, 'I told him to stuff it up his arse.' And what was more was that he believed it himself.

ELEVEN

Danny's manager was pacing around the room-a-like hotel suite like an expectant father on speed. Everything in the decor was muted and neutral to keep you calm and chilled, but it just wasn't working.
'What did you think you were doing? Are you mental?'
Danny hadn't seen Peter angry before and it was quite a scary sight. He was used to sycophancy from his manager not parental rage.
'I made a joke, what's the big deal?'
'It was the Kids Comedy Awards, Danny, you knew that.'
'I know.'
'It was a religious, terrorist, paedophile, paraplegic, joke.'
'But it was funny.'
'I'm not laughing. And you may not care about that Danny, but the BBC isn't laughing and neither is the film production company all the way over in the U.S of fucking A. Neither is the insurance company that we took so much money off to be their safe pair of hands. Those fuckers, the insurance guys, want to sue you because you went out there as their comedy persona, dressed as a strawberry, and now the internet is alive with what they are calling, "your filthy mouth"'.
'It was a lemon, a comedy lemon. It's a subtle difference but the lemon is a bitter, acidic fruit."
"Lemon, strawberry, whatever, they aren't dirty.'
At first Danny had started out feeling like a rebellious pirate, ready to shout 'fuck you' at anyone who challenged his comedy instincts, but now the pressure was building he was starting to think that maybe it had gone a little too far.
The incident had started quite innocently, he'd been rapping on camera with some kid who'd won the award for the longest continuous list of knock, knock jokes and it just ran away with him. The temptation to be totally outrageous had possessed him. The comedy in the moment of saying the

unsay-able in the place where it shouldn't be said was as funny to him as farting in church. Consequences had not been in his mind at that point.

'It was just a fucking joke Peter.'

'You don't do jokes about fucking on a kid's show.'

'It wasn't live, they cut it anyway.'

'The audience was live, there were kids in the audience and the footage is out there on YouTube. This sort of thing spreads faster than flu.'

'Ok, calm down Peter, it will blow over.'

'And if it doesn't? Do you realise the kind of earnings you have jeopardised with one smart comment? The BBC are re-looking at the sit-com, they are so frightened of taking risks they're over there now wondering if they made the right choice with you. Same thing with the movie people, it was offensive to them and they are shocked. They don't care what the British public thinks but they do care what the backers think.'

'And some of them are terrorist paedophiles?'

Peter ignored him, his anger wasn't going to break down on a joke.

'They didn't like the joke, OR where you chose to tell it.'

Danny was getting bored with being told off and frankly had expected more support from his manager.

'Well if it doesn't blow-over guess what, I'll still be a cult, I'll still have an audience.'

'Do you know what cult pays, compared to mainstream?'

'Why is it all about money with you Peter? Can't you see the art?'

'Art? Art? Don't make me laugh. Do you know what Damien Hirst charges for a pickled fish Danny? It's all about money you selfish, self-absorbed moron.'

Danny was now feeling like he was being very personally heckled and he did not like it at all. He was starting to feel very vulnerable, his armour of popularity suddenly stripped away. He was transported to that crushing first gig. Did you ever escape the pain of the first gig?

Peter sat down on the edge of the bed breathing heavily through his nose and Danny knew he had to wait until the red mist had cleared.
'So, are you saying that's it?' he asked at last. 'Is that it for me, my time is up, game over?'
'No, I didn't say that.' Peter was much calmer now. His role model in management was Colonel Tom Parker, Elvis's manager, who kept him in some kind of mysterious artistic strangle hold until all the money was made. 'I have to do some work and you have to do some apologising and shutting up.' He pointed at his own chest. 'I'm good, very good but you've really cut my work out for me this time. Still, you leave it with me. Talk to no journalists until I can set a few things up. I'll try to save your hide, but Danny, you're going to owe me big style.'

When the noise beeped and the red arrow flashed Steven walked forward and handed the brown envelope across the counter in the post office. Kevin had been helpful, supportive and encouraging, he'd told him where to send his sit-com, what to write in the letter, what names to drop and wished him luck. But it wasn't about luck, it was all about talent although that didn't stop Steven from keeping his fingers crossed for a full minute after he'd walked away.

When Steven got back to his office everyone was crowded around Adam's screen. He didn't push into the crowd, it was usually a piss-poor YouTube moment that the younger members of the team were sharing. The little group of happy colleagues all laughed and groaned in unison. Adam looked up from the front of the throng.
'Hey Steve, did you hear about this thing with Danny Childs the comedian?'
'Um, I heard something on the news, he offended someone?'
'He did this really rough joke on a kid's award ceremony in front of the Queen or something. Disgusting. It's on

YouTube, it's awful. I normally like him, but even I was gob smacked. He should be made to apologise live on TV. He should be banned, man. What was he thinking? They get so up themselves these comedians.'

'Steven looked over Adam's shoulder, but he had no way of knowing that the frozen image he could see was of the heckler who had all but ended Chicken's own comedy career back in Scarborough. He couldn't make the connection because he hadn't ever really seen him in the audience and he wouldn't have remembered him anyway.

Before the video had run Steven saw Katy beckoning him from within her glass walled office box. He left the kids to their comedy and went and sat down in Katy's comfortable chair. She was smiling. He'd never had any bad news from Katy but he was always a little wary that there might be some on its way. Things had been going so well in his corporate world that he wouldn't have been surprised by a vicious backlash. He didn't like to admit it but a part of him, a perverse, self-destructive hidden part craved the action of a bust up.

'Steve, look I want to run something by you. You've been working hard, putting in some extra hours and I appreciate that but the thing is we're going to be taking on a couple of new clients. I can't say too much about it at the moment but they are big. Actually they are huge.' Steven felt his rectum contract, and a swimming sickness in his stomach, surely this was Katy's lead up to telling him he wasn't up to the job and he was therefore on his way out. Suddenly he really, really didn't want the drama of a bust up, he wanted a quiet lie down instead. 'So,' she continued, 'I want you to grow the department, I think you need to hire another at least another two bodies. I want you Steven to do less of the work and more of the managing. I want you to be getting out of here on time of a night, so I think you need more support. I'd hate to lose you. How does that sound?'

'Good Katy, very good. It would be good to see a bit more of Laura and the baby.'

'Of course.'
Inside Steven felt more than a little guilty. His extra work had all been comedy script related. Added to this naughty uneasiness was the thought that once his sit-com script got picked up then he'd be leaving for good. In fact he'd already started mapping out his resignation letter.
'Well it's great for Zingtastic, Katy. I'm not sure who these new clients are but I'm just so pleased to be part of it.'
'And we're pleased to have you here Steven. I have to say I wasn't sure that you'd adjust to life after freelancing, not everyone can hack the old nine to five, but you've fitted in really well, and your work has been first rate. So, it's onward and upward.'
Steven took his cue and left Katy's office but as he did he wondered if he'd missed his chance to ask for a raise.

A miscalculation of travel arrangements had meant that Morgan arrived early at the Cha-cha club in Nottingham so he had some time to kill. He made his way to the bar located at the back of the slowly filling club. A young comedian introduced himself as one of the open spots for the night and Morgan taking pity offered to buy him a drink.
'Should I drink? Before I go on?'
'As much as possible.'
'You're Morgan aren't you?'
'Yes, I am.'
'One of my mates saw you the other night. In Birmingham.'
'Is he here? Because it's exactly the same act every night so if he is here he's seen it.'
'No, he isn't.'
They sat and had a couple of pints, the youngster getting more and more nervous while Morgan scanned the crowd for any problem punters. The kid started to talk rapidly to ease his nerves.
'Be great to be on TV wouldn't it. Have you done any TV?'
'A bit. I had a TV pilot once, a few years ago. BBC put fifty grand into it and then it disappeared, that's the way it goes.'

'What was it about?'
'Oh, me travelling round the country, taking a look at wacky Britain. It was going to be called Grey Britain.'
'It sounds a bit like that show that Harry Steadford does. Britain's Underbelly. That's good. Have you seen it?'
'Yeah. Yeah, I've seen it.'
They sat quietly for a few minutes.
'It's hard getting gigs though, when you're new like me.'
'Well, the only way to get good is to do lots of gigs. You need to do 200 gigs this year and then build on that.'
'200. That's a lot. I'd struggle to find that many. Do you have an agent?'
'Not any more. Used to, Matty Carlo? You won't have heard of him but then I thought why am I paying you twelve percent to book gigs that I can book myself? Clubs ring *me* up. I do alright. Unfortunately, I lost Jollysters. I used to have a regular booking there in three of their city venues but when I did the pilot I had to let them down on a few gigs. They don't like being told you can't make it so they never booked me ever again. Shame, because it was decent money and regular but there you are.'
'Right.I wouldn't be able to get a gig at Jollysters yet?'
'No. They have to invite you. It's like being scouted for a football team. Unfortunately I've been dropped. But there are loads of clubs out there now, more than when I started. There's also loads more comedians though. Too many comedians, that's the core of the problem. Too many shit comedians. Still, I'm sure you're brilliant.'
Morgan carried on drinking but the young fella stopped. The boy's nervousness had reached a level of very real pain that he could hardly bear, his body hurt and he was really suffering, wondering if he could say even one word let alone his carefully practised new act. When he was introduced he took a massively deep breath and walked forward and after his five minutes of patchy laughs he left the stage to a smattering of applause .

'Yes, that was fine.' said Morgan. 'Hang about and when I've finished I'll scribble down some numbers of promoters for you.'

He waited at the back to watch the mighty Morgan. The seasoned performer ambled out, slightly drunk but still funny. He worked the crowd and crushed all dissenters. The audience didn't seem to care that he was pissed, it sort of made him one of them, and he wasn't missing any punch lines. The kid watched and could see a future crystallising before his eyes. It was a job no more and no less. But was it a job that he wanted? Out every night? That awful sick nervous feeling? Fridays and Saturdays always busy? What about a family life? What about going out with your mates? And how much did it pay? Morgan didn't look rich.

Before Morgan had finished his set the kid had slipped away.

For Ray taking control of his string of hotel comedy clubs, his empire, had not quite worked out the way he'd thought it would, not at all in fact. The thing Ray hadn't factored in was that a cruise ship has a captive audience who can go nowhere while they go places. A club was a different entity. A club has to compete with all the other things that you can find to do that are more comfortable and cheaper. For the market that Ray had wanted the sheer inconvenience of getting out of the house at night was a hurdle. Somehow, for all his casual lack of professionalism Davis had a skill for coaxing punters in. He worked at it, every second of the day and since Ray had replaced him the gates had fallen dramatically. It wasn't about profit, it never had been, it was about keeping a life in those hotels when the rest of the world was asleep. It was about marketing and branding.

For Ray there were no problems only challenges and he surveyed his options. Of course he could sack his new entertainments manager and ask Davis to come back, but that felt too much like a climb-down. No, he needed fresh thinking. He knew it was time to be bold. He was going to fire the new entertainments guy, but he was going to sack comedy too. Comedy was over for the Rio Grand and all other associated hotels. It just didn't have the older punters appeal that he'd hoped for. He had big ideas though and they had come to him while he'd been watching a documentary on Las Vegas. Cards, mature punters like cards, and a hotel was a perfect venue for a huge glittering Bridge Centre. Bridge, rummy and whist. That was the bold new future. Forget comedy.

'Can you let me out now? I've finished.' She shook her head, although from inside the box he couldn't see her do it. She tapped on the top of the box with her long red nails.
'Finished? Without me? You naughty boy. I think you might need to spend a little more time helpless in there.' He rattled at the door and she sat on it.
'Honestly, um, it's getting a bit hot in here now.'
'You do love honesty don't you? Of course it's getting hot, you're in a box.'
'But I really need to get out now.'
'I decide when you get out Thomas. It might be when I think you are ready to give me a raise Thomas, and I'm not talking about your cock. Who knows?'
'Elizabeth?'
'Yes?'
'Are you blackmailing me Elizabeth?'
'No, I'm keeping you helpless Thomas, helpless until I get what I want. Like I did before to get the job I wanted. Do you realise how helpless you are Thomas?'
There was a rhythmic rocking from the box beneath her and a low satisfied groan.
'Elizabeth?'
'What Thomas?'
'I love you Elizabeth, you're the only one who has ever understood me.'
'Oh, I don't understand you Thomas. She said, unhooking the clasp to let him out. 'I just know how to make you do what I want.'

He got back from work quite early after leaving on time as he usually did these days but his good mood evaporated immediately he saw the thick wedge of a package on the kitchen table. He took off his shoes, walked slowly over and with hands braced against the table stood and stared at it for at least a minute before taking it unopened and putting it in a drawer. Later when Laura asked him if he'd seen his letter he grunted that he'd open it later and she was too busy on baby duties to question it. He'd heard that acceptances come in thin letters and rejections are heaving great fat bastards of bundled up returned work. He tried to put it out of his mind but he didn't succeed.

Sadly Steven thought about the phone call he'd had the day before, a totally unexpected catch-up from Morgan. They hadn't spoken since the night he'd dropped him off after the late night drive back from York. It had shocked him to hear Morgan's voice and it took a fair bit of aimless chatter from the usually abrupt comedian before Steven could work out why he'd rung. Morgan had been to York again, and stayed with Kevin the writer again, and Kevin had mentioned that Steven was writing a sit-com. He must have really bigged it up because Morgan's sole reason for reigniting the friendship was to see if there might be a role in the script for him. Sighing heavily Steven had explained that he was just the writer, that it had only been accepted for reading by one of Kevin's contacts and that it was a long, long way from casting, NOT that a writer would get much say in that anyway. Steven felt a little disappointed that he'd allowed himself to be drawn in by Morgan and had even flirted with the idea that perhaps the git actually had something interesting for *him*. In fact all he wanted was that elusive television escape hatch into the enchanted land of the famous. Any trailing string of possibility was enough to get Morgan clutching.

'Come on Chicken, we've shared some times, you can pull a few strings for me. Remember, we shared a B and B mate and we shared a stage in York.'
'I didn't get a gig in York, Morgan.'
'Didn't you?'
'No, Morgan. I didn't.'
The blind self interest didn't surprise Steven really, Morgan spent his entire life travelling from gig to gig fighting to be the centre of attention. Drive into town, be the one in the spot light and then drive to the next gig.

Late in the night baby Heather began crying and Steven was already awake staring at the ceiling so he patted his stirring wife and went to fetch his daughter from her cot. Some of the baby manuals said not to do it, instead to let them cry until they went back to sleep, but there were too many tears in the world for Steven right now. He picked up his writhing daughter, cradled her on his shoulder and went slowly down the stairs to pace with her.
The house was quiet and there were no noises in the street, not even the bass thumps of the cars that idled sometimes outside their neighbour's house. He walked with Heather who was now calm, but he didn't want to put her down, he was enjoying the light weight of her warm body on his neck. He felt as if he was protecting her, keeping her safe and warm and she in turn was making him feel needed.
He went to the drawer, and awkwardly with his left hand he took out the package, placed it back on the table and then without any further waiting ripped it open. He scanned the letter that was enclosed with his sit-com manuscript. He saw,..*lot of promise...good touches of humour...nice characterisation...sorry...unfortunately...if you write anything else.*
It was a rejection as he'd known it was when he'd smelled it from the doorway, but even knowing it was coming didn't dull the disappointment.

'Shit,' he whispered, and then remembering his sleeping daughter on his shoulder swallowed the worse words that wanted to spill out. He felt utterly deflated. It was exactly the reason why he hadn't wanted to open the letter in front of Laura. It would have been perfect, an unexpected lottery win if it had been successful, but not this way. He'd have had to explain about the script and when he'd found time to write it. The late nights when he could have been home instead of sitting typing a failed script at work. And then Laura would have read words like 'lots of promise' in the letter and she'd have thought that they were good words. None of it was good. They could say it was a work of genius but if they still rejected it for some reason or another then it was a waste. He didn't want to hear that it was good, he'd have preferred to be told that he had no chance and that it was rubbish. Now he was left with that trailing half promise that there was a chance if he happened to write anything else.

He began to pace again with Heather. In the front room he considered turning on the TV. On the coffee table was a DVD of Chazbatz, one of Heather's favourites, a painful children's show that featured lots of running, shouting, and custard pies. He glanced at the cover. Even beneath the ridiculous farmer's costume he recognised a face from the comedy circuit. He couldn't remember the guy's name but he'd obviously done pretty well to have graduated to throwing gunge at children instead of insults at drunks. He couldn't bear to watch any forced comedy so he walked with Heather and talked to her softly.

'I used to be a comedian. Yep, unbelievable isn't it. I used to stand up on stage in front of people and try to make them laugh. Sometimes they did and sometimes they didn't. If I was still doing that I probably wouldn't be walking around with you tonight, I'd be driving back from some gig somewhere. On my own, in the dark. Of course I would have most of the day to be with you but I wouldn't be here at night. And most weekends I'd be busy.' He kept his voice comforting and sing-song. 'But I gave it up, not really because I wanted to, it's just that I couldn't make enough money really. You need money for little things like food and clothes, so I got a proper job. In a design studio where I draw pictures all day, which sounds like fun, but in fact I don't really draw them I just make sure other people are doing their drawings. Obviously Heather, there's more to it than that but I'm trying to keep it simple for you. So, to keep me from screaming at the same time I tried to write a TV comedy script. That's it there on the table. That big fat thing. But no one wanted it babe. I thought I could make a lot of money. Enough for all our food and clothes, but maybe not. Now I could try to send it to other people who make telly programmes like Chazbatz, I could try to rewrite it and I could try and try to find someone who liked it. But I don't think I'm going to do that. I could also try to write a new one. Think up another idea and then sit late at work and try to write another one, but it's exhausting and soul destroying Heather, it really is. And it's disappointing when no one wants it at the end.'

He stopped talking and sighed and then listened to the silence of the house. He suddenly felt that if it wasn't for Heather clinging to his shoulder he would be so alone it would kill him. He would die, die on the stage of life. 'I'm not sure that I can keep doing that job Heather, all that kept me going in there was the thought that soon I'd be doing something better. But now there isn't a better, now I know that's the limit. So what I have to do is have a thing called a reality check. I have to stop torturing myself with unattainable dreams. So that's what I'm going to do. Stop. Really stop. I'm going to stop trying to make comedy that no one wants and I'm going to do a job, that if I'm honest Heather loads of people would kill for. I've got nothing to moan about, not really, I'm just going to get on with it.' He turned, half expecting to see Laura standing behind him listening in the doorway, but in fact in the quiet he could hear her softly snoring upstairs.

He took the manuscript and dropped it into the bottom of the bin. Then he took his daughter back up to her bed. He stood over her cot until he was sure that she was sleeping soundly, whispered that he loved her then crept from the room to slide back into the now cold bed. His wife snaked out a hand to hold his.
'Is she ok?' she asked sleepily.
'Yes.' He whispered. 'She's fine and she's beautiful.' and then too quietly for
Laura to hear he added, 'but I'm not sure about me.'

TWELVE

'And I'm really sorry.' Danny was saying to the earnest interviewer on the nationally broadcast current affairs show, *Word to the Wise*. 'Sometimes a comedian's mouth runs away with him, and that's what happened there.'
'Now we can't specifically detail the so called joke Danny, we aren't allowed to due to its inappropriate nature, but I have to ask you. You didn't just do it in a cynical move to get publicity for your tour?'
'The tour's finished Bob,' he smiled. 'And besides, who needs hate mail publicity? My postman has had to start wearing protective gloves. He hates me as well, he's throwing my mail at me these days.'
'Some of the kids who were there Danny, at the awards, are still traumatised by what you said. We talked to one mother who said her son cried himself to sleep that night. You'd been such a hero to him before.'
Danny had to literally bite his tongue until the pain cut through his desire to laugh out loud. The myriad things that he wanted to say to that fought for space in his mouth. He breathed deeply and struggled to control himself. Surely there was only so much shit that a comedian had to take. What was he a man or a PR arse licker? He coughed. He held his breath, he knew that guffawing was not an option and he didn't dare speak because that's what would happen. Bob was staring at him, at last the interviewer said in a more sympathetic tone than he'd had before,
'Well I can see that you are moved by that Danny, so maybe it has come home to you just how much responsibility you have as a public figure. And now over to David at the war protests and riots that are happening in four of our major cities today.'

Laura turned off the TV set as she was clearing up after the breakfast with Heather, who was sitting happily in her high-

chair as if plastered in a porridge explosion. She was scraping out some of the breakfast into the bin when she saw the packet in the bottom and recognised it as the one that had arrived for Steve the day before. He never told her what it was and she was only mildly curious, knowing that it would be some kind of junk mail but she couldn't understand why he hadn't put it in the recycling. She pulled it out and wiped the porridge off. The front was ripped open and although it wasn't addressed to her she could read the letter. She sat down opposite happy Heather.
'Oh Steve,' she said to herself, 'you poor soul. Why didn't you tell me?'
Once Heather was changed and the nanny had arrived to take her out to the park so that Laura could work, she sat in her make-shift office, the one in the kitchen that had been Steve's when he was freelance and read through the forty pages, smiling and laughing from time to time. She put the script in the bottom drawer of her desk. It infuriated her, he was such a wimp, he'd written this excellent script but after one rejection he'd binned it. What he needed was someone to sell it for him, someone who would treat it impartially and not take rejection personally, someone who was thick-skinned enough to keep pushing on the doors that wouldn't open. She only knew one person like that. She picked up the phone and began to call her network.
'Carrie, hi, it's me. Yes, great, listen are you still a media whore? Fantastic, look out of interest if I was selling a comedy TV script who would I send it to? Really, wonderful, email me that list please.'
Laura thought about it. If she put aside a few hours a week to push Steven's script what was there to lose? If she brought her marketing and sales experience and her large network of contacts to bear on it as a project chances were she could get something out of it. She wasn't at all sure how much money there was to be made but now that the work was done and the very funny script was sitting in her drawer it was worth a shot.

Potty mouth or no potty mouth it was Danny's public crying that had finally turned public opinion back in his favour. It was the sight of him breaking down in the face of the pain and unhappiness that he had caused to young innocent kids that had swung it on the fickle barometer of love and hate. He hadn't been crying of course, he'd been fighting to prevent himself doing even more harm with another destructive comment. But it didn't matter, if he told the press that he hadn't been crying they simply wouldn't have believed him now. Danny didn't feel good about any of it. He didn't mind the world thinking that he'd been sobbing, although there was a small playground in his heart that felt a little shame, it was more about what it meant for his future as an artist.

Peter on the other hand was over the moon as the love was starting to come back. Media opportunities were starting to open up again. He kept telling Danny how happy he should be but Danny did not feel happy. It was true that his earning potential was reviving but something had been lost. Part of what Danny had revelled in was the fact that as a comedian he was beholden to no one. He said what he wanted when he wanted to and everyone laughed. He was a free spirit of rebellion and admired for his cheek. But now it turned out he was nowhere near as free as he thought. It reminded him of an old friend who had left a corporate position to start his own business and been initially ecstatic that he didn't have to answer to a boss anymore only to find after a few months that in fact the bank manager was his new boss. Like-wise Danny had discovered that he was a slave to the public, and worse the people he worked for were pretty thick. He was now answerable to everyone. He could be as rebellious as he liked as long as he stayed within the lines and if you were staying in the lanes how rebellious really was that?

Steven sat at his desk and looked unseeingly at the various very urgent emails that he'd been sent. Every day in the office was a series of crises to be solved, but nothing was touching him today. Karen came with a holiday request form and he signed it without even consulting the holiday chart. Emma came to ask if she could purchase some software and he signed that form too. Even Adam picked up on the vibe and arrived with a print-out of a two day training course. Steven signed his third form in ten minutes. He was aware that paperwork that you agree without due diligence always comes back to bite your arse, but he was beyond caring. If this was now going to be his career until he died then he should be paying more attention but the opposite was true. He couldn't see the point. He was grieving for a dead script and he couldn't even bring himself to look at the folder on his desktop where its ghost still remained.

He noticed that Adam was still hovering at his desk.

'Did you see that grovelling apology from Danny Childs? What a dick.'

'Who?'

'The comedian that I showed you on YouTube, the one who did that joke in front of the kids?'

'Oh, right. Yes.'

'He had to apologise, and then, HE CRIED. In an interview. Oh, man. It's was harsh. What a wimp.'

Steven didn't point out that only days before Adam like the rest of the interested public had been baying for an apology.

'Maybe he's had enough.'

'Yeah, but he's a comedian, that's his job, he should have just stuck two fingers up at the lot of 'em. He should have made a joke twice as nasty and laughed in their faces.'

'Maybe he's just thinking that he can't take being beaten up for trying to make people laugh anymore? Maybe he's tired of it all?'

'Wimp,' and with that Adam started to walk away.

'You should try it Adam. The comedy game. Really, I think it would be great,' and then to himself Steven added, 'watching you get ripped to shit for committing the crime of trying to be funny.'

Steven was sitting playing with Heather on the mat in the time slot before her bath, book and bed. Laura looked over at the splash of primary colours made by Heather's chunky plastic toys.

'Steve. Why didn't you tell me that you'd been writing a comedy script?' he looked at her quizzically. 'I saw it in the bin and I thought you'd forgotten to recycle again.'

'I didn't think you'd be interested Laura.'

'But it's really good.'

'No it's not. It's rejected by people who know what they are talking about.'

'But they said it had promise.'

'Yes. So much promise that they didn't want it.'

'You could send it to other people. Maybe there are other people who know more than the people that you've already tried.'

'Look, I appreciate your support love, but I don't want to talk about it. It's over and it's time for me to forget all that.'

'Fine. But would you mind if I sent it out?'

'Why?'

'Because I think it's really funny, and I can't help thinking that so will someone else.'

'Laura, you're great at your job and everything but this isn't your area. Do you know what it takes to get a script onto television? Do you have any idea how many writers spend their whole lives trying? It was stupid of me to even attempt it.'

'I understand. But would you mind?'

'Be my guest. As long as you do me a favour. Keep the rejections away from me. No matter how much promise they say it has and no matter how complimentary, if it's a rejection it's a rejection and I don't want to know.'

THIRTEEN

It was three months now since Laura had taken on the job of trying to get a deal for Steven's script and she had to admit to more than a little frustration. She'd spent every Wednesday morning concentrating on the world of media in its many grimy forms and it was starting to get her down. For an industry built on fast moves and shiny performances show business was proving to be a very, very slow business. It seemed to take an age for anyone to answer any sort of communication at all. It was like trying to push a ten ton truck through an ocean of treacle. She began to wonder how television programmes ever got made at all. How did executives who never return calls or send emails ever make the wheels turn? There seemed to be no urgency anywhere in the system. Coming from a background of desperate software sales where urgency was all there ever was she was struggling to understand what she was fighting against. There was nothing for Laura to get her claws into and her lack of experience in the field left her open to some very patronising comments. It was a closed shop, a cosy club with unspoken rules and her belief that selling a script should be the same as punting a can of beans had taken a dent. Maybe Steven was right, maybe it was beyond her skill set. However, she wasn't ready to give up yet and while she still had some friends on her side supplying her with names, numbers and email addresses she was prepared to keep pushing. There was a caveat to her continued commitment though, she was beginning to think that perhaps she ought to spend just a little more of her emotional effort in turning in work for the growing list of other contacts and clients who made her feel wanted and loved in the best way; in short the ones who paid.

It was three months now since Steven had agreed to take on more staff to make his job easier, and strangely it had made his job harder. It wasn't going well, he wasn't really coping with the whole management side of things. It was the small things that he hated like deciding who could go on holiday and when. It was also the big things such as who would do the jobs as they came into the studio. His choices had come into question when it started to look like some of the designers had an easier ride than others. It wasn't true, he wasn't playing favourites he simply wasn't organised enough to track whose turn it was to have an easy job. It was leading to stress. Steven had thought that nothing could be as nerve wracking as waiting to go on stage, but it wasn't true. The constant pressure of the office was wrecking his sleep far more than late nights in grotty pub clubs ever had. Generally he was dealing with the increased pressure by tuning out and shoving important paperwork to the back of his desk where it could be lost behind his computer. His lack of concentration and generally lax attitude was beginning to back-fire on him and the company. Katy had stopped smiling through the glass at him. One of the prestigious new clients had fallen away. It was no one's fault but it felt like his. Some work had slipped through unchecked and mistakes had made it all the way to print. He had no one to off-load the blame onto so he'd had to take it himself and he knew that was probably his greatest management failing: getting caught without a scapegoat.

It was three months now since Danny had grovelled his way back into the good books of the nation. Most of the public had forgotten his transgression and moved on. Every day his image grew stronger and every day he felt a little bit worse inside. His manager was pulling all the strings, especially the ones attached to the purse, he was booking the gigs and arranging the schedule and all Danny had to do was turn up and be funny in a not too threatening way. Being funny was getting harder but it didn't seem to matter, the crowds laughed anyway. It was as if they had been programmed to accept him as a comedian so they listened in that context.

He didn't know why he was feeling so uncomfortable with it all but it was probably because he was thinking about it too much. So many people had told him over a long time that comedy doesn't stand analysis and he knew it was true, but when he stared hard at what it was that made many people laugh he started to lose sight of why he'd ever wanted to be a comedian. 'It's just funny or it isn't' no longer answered it for him. He had the secret now, he knew how to make people laugh and he just had to continue to play the game. He just had to pander to their needs, to give them what they wanted and expected. He just had to be a funny puppet.

Laura took the call from her friend Carrie even though it was a Thursday afternoon, which wasn't strictly her 'Steve's script' time but she handled it anyway. Calls coming in on that project were so rare that she would have taken one at any time.
Carrie said that she had some good friends over from L.A., a couple who were involved somehow in the movie business and she wanted permission to show them the script. As she put it, 'They're like roving talent scouts and they're always grilling me for new ideas, new angles anything English that they might be interested in and all I've got at the moment is that script.'
'Okay. Sounds good. Do they make T.V. shows?'
'No.'
'So can it help?'
'How can it hurt?'
'You're right. What the hell.'
'Well, the last thing they took off me went well. Do you remember that film with Hugh Grant? The Cryptic English Garden?'
'That?'
'Yes, that was one of theirs that they made from a script I gave them.'
'Okay, well thanks Carrie, and let's keep our fingers crossed.'

It was typical of the conversations that Laura had been having lately regarding Steven's work. Pointless.

'We need to talk Steven.'
He was in Katy's office again, but the atmosphere had changed noticeably from its previously friendly slant.
'They are taking the piss.' Katy was pointing at the office on the other side of her glass wall. 'You are letting them take liberties, and because they are young and dumb that's exactly what they are doing. They come in here with no real appreciation of what a deadline really means. They are little more than children. And that's why I hired you Steven. You have to show through experience, wisdom and arse kicking why clients can't be let down and work has to be done. YouTube is not work.'
'Well, you know we try to promote a creative vibe here Katy. We want them to be happy in their work and do great things because of it. Like Microsoft or Google or one of those funky American companies.'
'In those companies Steven, they play hard and they work hard. They work long into the night. Here they come in at ten thirty or eleven, they piss off for lunch at twelve and they just about make it back in time to go home.'
'But Katy, they...' Katy was holding up her hand.
'No. Sort it out Steven before I do. I did your wife a favour when I took you on, but friendship only goes so far.'
Steven sat up.
'You did what?'
'I gave you a chance Steven, don't let me down.'
'Did you say that you took me on as a favour?'
'Can we just focus on the job in hand Steven?' She pointed at Adam who was throwing screwed up paper balls at Lucy's head. It did look like a school playground out there in the design studio. It might have made a good scene if Steven's sit-com had ever come to anything. Steven stood up.
'I'll go and ring the bell for the end of break.'
Katy didn't laugh, or even smile.

'Yes, you do that Steven, and let's review the situation in a week. Let's see if you have any more control by then.'

The promoter was young, fresh and nervous and glowing with the eagerness of the new club. Morgan on the other hand was long in the tooth and seething inside. He could see exactly how this was going to pan out. There had been no promotion, not even a poster on the door upstairs to say that there would be a comedy show down there tonight. It was going to be a disaster. There were just four people sitting at a table near the back and three more scattered around the room and it was only fifteen minutes to show time. The other two comedians were sitting in silent disappointment. They were looking to Morgan as the experienced headliner for his reaction so he was keeping a detached air. He stood and wandered upstairs to the bar. As he was about to order he was joined at his side by the young promoter who grinned agitatedly.
'I think it's because of the England game that's on telly tonight,' he said. 'Everyone is staying home.'
'Could be.'
'I had a bit of a set back with the emails that I should have sent out as well. Basically they didn't get sent.'
'And the posters?'
'Yeah, my mate was going to do some posters, but y'know, he's been a bit busy.'
Morgan looked at him and his stupid grin. He was a stoner and a piss artist and Morgan had seen it all before. Running a club had looked easy to him no doubt. He'd booked the room, hired the comedians with weeks to spare and then all of a sudden he'd seen the ground rushing up towards him.
'Yep, it's going to be a quiet night,' Morgan said.
'So as I was relying on the takings on the door to pay the comedians and ...'
Morgan held up a finger.
'Not my problem,' he said. 'Don't tell me about things that are not my problem. You booked me to do the gig and once

I've done my forty minutes to that empty room you owe me two hundred quid.'
Panic was gripping the lad. 'But I...'
'Not my problem. You should thank me, you've just learned a lesson. If you're going to run a club you have to get your head out of your arse.'
'You want two hundred. What about the other two?'
'I don't give a fuck about those two you just need to worry about me.'
Much later when Morgan was driving back, his pocket bulging with a cheque that would surely bounce he began to laugh. All alone, driving through the night in the yellow of the street lights he laughed more than he'd laughed in weeks. After all these years it was the sheer amateurishness of his professional life that was pushing him into a despair that could only result in hysteria. What was he going to do? How long could he keep this up?

Danny's career had been rebuilt to the point where he could now be booked into reasonably large venues again and Peter was sounding him out on who he wanted to use as a warm up.
'You don't want them to steal the show,' he was saying, 'but you don't want them to bum the audience out either.'
'Morgan. Get in touch with Morgan.'
'Never heard of him.'
'He's a circuit professional and he'll do the job. Besides, I'd like to catch up with him again.'
Danny knew that Morgan would never remember him as the heckler in Scarborough, chances were that he wouldn't even remember the gig, but Danny remembered and for him it had become an item of unfinished business.
'How will I find him?'
'Come on Peter, for fuck's sake, you're the man with the plan, you're the manager. Should be easy, he's not Osama Bin laden, you know, when he was still alive, Morgan won't be living in a remote cave somewhere.' He thought about

that. It depended how things had been going for him of course, by now Morgan might well be living rough.

She stopped looking at her screen and started to pay some attention to the phone cradled in her neck and shoulder. It was a habit that gave her a stiff neck but she couldn't help it and lapsed into the position without even noticing.
'Are you sure about this Carrie? No, it's just that it sounds like a wind up. Ok. Ok. I'll leave it with you.'
After putting down the phone she sat back and shook her head slowly. Amazing, she thought. If it was true it was the most incredible thing she'd ever heard, but still, being a businesswoman she was aware that she should wait for the email before letting the flutter of excitement take hold of her stomach. Besides, she still had plenty of work to do on this project.

Something was in the air in the design studio and Steven was being buffeted by a paranoia that he never even knew he had. Where was his 'don't give a shit' attitude when he needed it? He'd been making a coffee in the communal kitchen area and Katy, the boss, had come in to get some iced water. She hadn't smiled and she hadn't looked him in the eye. It probably meant nothing and he was just being stupid but he was sure that there was an invisible something seeping through the office. It was true that they'd lost another big client but these things happened in business. It was a bad run that much was clear but not all of it could be laid at Steven's door. A couple of the new designers that he'd hired were proving to be highly creative and very effective, so he was taking credit for that. They were getting through the work, and now that Steven had explained to them all that if they didn't stop acting like kids in an adventure playground they might be back in one, they had got their acts together. There was the little incident where three people had gone on holiday for the same week leaving them a little under resourced, but Steven had smoothed that over with Katy. All in all, he really didn't have anything to feel vulnerable about, so why did he? And then he figured it out, it was the iced water. Katy always drank coffee in the morning, but obviously she didn't want to stand and have a full conversation with him in the kitchen while she made herself a cup, so she'd grabbed a quick glass of water instead. And that wasn't paranoia, that was logic worthy of Sherlock Holmes.

FOURTEEN

Morgan made his way to the theatre where he was due to meet the latest comedy sensation, Danny Childs and his manager, Peter. It had been a strange few days but Morgan had a good feeling about this latest development. In his cynical world it was rare for Morgan to have less than a foreboding about anything on the horizon, so it was a rare occurrence to have a meeting that he wasn't dreading. It had started with a call from Matty Carlo, Morgan's sacked agent whom he hadn't spoken to for quite some time, not since Morgan had told him to go fuck himself anyway. Morgan had taken the whimpering collapse of his fledgling television career very badly and of course there had to be someone to blame other than himself. Matty had been that person and he probably wouldn't even have taken this latest call from him but for the fact that he'd deleted Matty's number a year before and now he didn't recognise it.
As soon as Morgan had picked up Matty the battle hardened agent had dived in like a kingfisher and got right to the point as though they'd never had a cross word. Remembering some of the things that he'd launched at Matty in the past Morgan was left marvelling at skin that was less like a rhinoceros and more like the walls of a nuclear bunker.
'Morgan, good to talk to you, they want you. They love you and they are very, very keen to talk to you. And it's a big theatre.'
As an introduction it was clever, no matter how much bad blood had flowed between them above all else Morgan wanted to be wanted. Matty knew that because Matty was well aware of just how shallow an entertainer's waters run. That's why he'd used the L word too. They all needed to be wanted, loved and pampered like babies.
'Matty. What are you talking about?'
Now that Morgan was hooked Matty could afford to expand a little and at the same time paint himself into the picture

where he currently only featured as a vague sketch. 'I've had a call from an old mate. Don't ask. We go way, way back.' He actually didn't know Peter and probably had never met him, but they knew some of the same people, which to Matty was exactly the same thing. 'This mate is the manager of a comedian called Danny Childs. Young pup, you won't have heard of him.'

'I've heard of him.'

Matty was in pushing mode so he wasn't really listening. 'Childs has got some big theatre gigs booked all over the place and they're looking for warm-ups. I managed to squeeze you into the frame. It pays well and it's good exposure. They want to talk to you.'

The truth was that at Danny's request Peter had put out some feelers for Morgan and Matty's name had come up on an outdated internet database as his agent.

Morgan closed his eyes. Warm-up to some kid who'd been in the business for a fraction of the time that Morgan had been staggering along the highways of comedy. It didn't appeal much, but still it could be the chance to get in front of some large audiences, and just because they came to see Danny Childs it didn't mean that they wouldn't go away talking about the excellent warm-up. And besides, Danny Childs was crawling with TV interest, even if he'd tried to blow himself out of the water with that YouTube thing which in Morgan's opinion was the best thing he'd ever done. Letting go on a kid's TV show, now that was funny. Still, even though he was ready to work with Danny Childs, which would be better than the Dog and Duck where he was booked this weekend, there was still a ritual to go through with Matty.

'Thing is Matty, I'm pretty busy at the moment.'

Matty hadn't forgotten *everything* that had passed between them and he wasn't about to take any shit this time around. 'Don't dick me around Morgan, they can get warm-ups acts anywhere. Just get down to the Alarma Theatre in Putney by

five o'clock and hope to god that they like you. I've done my best, now don't let yourself down.'
Matty wasn't letting on but he was very sure that they would like him because they had hunted Morgan down. He wasn't at all sure why, but it didn't matter, if there was a chance for Matty to oil a few wheels and make some money, why not?

It was four thirty and Morgan walked in through the foyer of the theatre. There was no one about but even for a jaded old hand like him it was thrilling. He took in the faded elegance and echoes of good times that had been had by generations of punters now long gone. He took a deep breath and thought, *this is where I should be by now. Way beyond the Dog and Duck. I should have mugs coming to my theatre to see my show.* One of his many opening lines flashed across his mind, *Hello, it's great to be here. By the way, where the fuck are we?* So many times there had been a massive chunk of truth in that line, but not here, not in a big proper theatre.

Morgan was starting to wonder if the whole thing had been an elaborate revenge wind-up by Matty when Danny came out from somewhere and greeted him warmly. They shook hands like grown-ups and then at Danny's suggestion went to sit in the theatre manager's office. Impressing even himself Morgan had actually done some homework by checking out some of Danny's stuff on the internet. He might have done better at school if all homework was as easy as that.
Comedian's were very rarely like their stage personas, having met so many Morgan was used to that and it was certainly true of Danny, who rather than the bouncing livewire came across in person as quiet and considered and even quite dull. He was a thinker and they always made Morgan feel uncomfortable. Right from the start Morgan felt he was being scrutinised but not in an interview or audition way, more like a creepy stalker style. Danny kept cocking his

head to one side and squinting as if trying to see him better. They talked about comedy a little bit and about the gigs that Danny had coming up and then quietly Danny asked Morgan how he felt about hecklers.

'Generally they are a pain in the arse,' he answered, 'but sometimes they help me to lift a show. You can turn them to your advantage.' He wasn't being truthful, they were always a pain to him but he didn't want to say anything that might count against him in this non-audition, non-interview situation.

'I've seen that,' said Danny.

'Yeah?'

'Do you remember a few years ago doing a gig up North in Scarborough?'

'I do the North East Coast every year, Dan. There are a few good gigs up that way.'

'Yeah, but do you remember doing a gig, where there was a real arse-hole heckler, and he ruined the guy's set who was on before you?'

'Not really, were you there?'

'I was. The comedian was called Chicken as I recall.'

'Oh, right. Chicken. What happened at the gig?'

'You came out like a real pro and you let rip. You slaughtered the heckler. You absolutely went to town. You left him lying in a pool of piss. It was hysterical.'

Danny was grinning widely. Some of it was ringing bells for Morgan, but not much. There had been a lot of gigs and a lot of beer since then. He vaguely remembered something about a TV opportunity, but he couldn't make it all come back clearly.

'Glad, you enjoyed it.'

'It was me. I was the heckler.' Danny was still grinning.

'You?' Morgan could see that this was true from the look in Danny's eye and he was wondering how cutting and abusive he'd been to the heckler. Did Danny have a knife behind his back?

'Long story but I had some issues let's say, and the only way I could resolve them was to shout at comedians.'
'Right. Well you seem to have turned that around. You're all over the TV now.'
'I always felt bad about it though Morgan, bad for Chicken, now I've seen it from the other side I mean.'
'Forget it. He's writing sit-coms now. You did him a favour. He should thank you.'
'And I should thank you Morgan. Don't worry, it's not an issue now, and it has given me an idea about lifting my show. I don't want to get stale just because I'm in the big rooms.'
'Ok.'
'I'm already disappointed Morgan at how stupid audiences can be.'
'Ok.'
'The things they will laugh at,' he shook his head, 'it's depressing sometimes. You don't need to be clever or ground breaking you just have to play the game.'
Morgan was not getting it. Either he had been asked to come along to be murdered or to act as a comedy counsellor but either way all he really wanted was well paid well attended gig.
'Well, funny's funny,' he managed to grin back.
'Not really. Stupid's funny a lot of the time. Anyway I have a plan. Basically, you do your forty minutes warm up, get the crowd going, tickle their ribs a bit and all that. Then when you come off you go back, behind the stage, round and out into the audience. Then, when I come on you throw some heckles at me. I've written them, you shout them out and I have some good come-backs. Also a couple of the things give me a lead-in to other material.'
'Ohhhh, right, got you. Is that all? Can't you get someone else to do that?'
'I could Morgan, of course, but this is so fitting. You were the one who woke me up when you showed me what a snivelling coward I was sitting there in the crowd when what I

wanted to be was up on stage. Now look at me, I make more in a month than you probably make in a year. But at that gig in Scarborough I saw you take the room to a new height with your vicious tongue. It's what they want to see and it's only right that it should be you that gets to heckle me.'
'Are you sure Danny?'
'You have to stick to the script though, you gotta give me things I'm ready for, but it will work. The audience will love it.'
'But they'll know it's me, they'll recognise me. I'll have just come off stage for Christ's sake?'
'It'll be dark out there Morgan and most of them won't even know where the shouts are coming from.'
Morgan nodded, but he hated the idea. It wasn't even new, comedians had been fielding pre-written heckles for years. It was lame in Morgan's opinion, it stank because the whole point of dealing with disturbances was the spontaneity of the answers. He wasn't about to jeopardise his new gig by telling Danny but it struck him as something you were more likely to see in a theatre than a comedy club. A big old fashioned theatre. Like this one.

One of the life advantages of being a lawyer was that it taught one to make practical emotionless decisions based on reasoned and logical assessment. It also trained one to read the small print, but that was just a tedious habit. Thomas Dalfin had thought long and hard about this and he was now ready to make his move. It was an intensely personal issue, but his main concerns were professional. How would Arthur Chase react? It was too important a question to leave to chance so he'd booked a meeting, laid out his case and run it by the most senior of partners. Thomas had been thorough and persuasive and when it came to the judgement in principle Arthur had raised no objections. There was the question of company policy, but Thomas was prepared for that and easily explained why that wouldn't be a problem. Job done. So now that he had cleared it with Arthur, Thomas was ready to put it to Elizabeth that he'd like to marry her.

She was perfect. It had been a revelation to Thomas just how content he'd become now that his needs were being met in the safety and comfort of his own home. She was inventive too and he could see that boredom was never going to smoother their relationship. Elizabeth knew what he wanted and she knew how to give it to him so he could easily imagine a life of utter happiness stretching out before him. He'd covered all the bases, even sounded out Jago Steller, celebrity chef to the stars on the possibility of him catering the wedding and so he was now ready to pop the question. Although he wasn't a barrister, Thomas stuck with the maxim that you should never ask a question that you didn't know the answer to and of course he knew the answer to this one. It was yes. Still, he found himself slightly nervous, it was a big moment. He wiped some sweat from his nose, took a shallow breath and blurted,

'Elizabeth I've given this a lot of consideration and on balance I'd like to ask you to marry me.'

Elizabeth was genuinely shocked. 'Did I hear you right? Can you say that again?'

'I'm asking you to marry me.'

Elizabeth pursed her lips and frowned. Men were so utterly pathetic. But it was a very interesting proposition and one that deserved some respect. She unsnapped the clasps on the hall cupboard and opened the door so she could look Thomas in the eye. She helped him out and then untied him and gave him his robe so that he could cover his nakedness. Whatever her answer she didn't want this to be an offer made under duress or in the nude.

'Well, well, well, I know we've been having fun Thomas, or at least you have, but what's brought this on?'

'Oh, I don't know, I guess I'm quite old fashioned really. We are so suited Elizabeth. Where would I ever find anyone who was so understanding and accepting of my lifestyle? It's been a miracle, I chose to be honest and fate brought you to me.'

'Fate?'

'Exactly. If you look at all great men who fall from grace what brings them down is their indiscretions. Men will risk absolutely anything to get the kind of sex that they want. I have a big career ahead of me Elizabeth, so if I can bring my passions in-house so that I never need to look outside I can protect myself.'

'That's romantic Thomas, but as you mentioned career I should point out that the problem is work Thomas. We work together.'

'My love, don't fret, I'm way ahead of you. I've already asked Arthur Chase and he said yes, go ahead with it.'

'Right, so you asked Arthur about marrying me before you asked me?'

'I needed to know that my job would be safe. Goodness, my career isn't fully established yet so I still need Steel & Caskett.'

'But I thought there was a company policy about married couples working together? Are you telling me crusty old Chase is willing to overlook that?'

'No, but that's the beauty of it my darling. Once we're married you won't need to work anymore. You'll be married. To me. You'll have all the money you need and a standard of living that is way beyond what you have now.'

'But I like working Thomas, what about my career? I'm the Head of Marketing for a large legal practice. It's a prestige position.'

He laughed. 'Oh come on Elizabeth, we both know how you got that role and it wasn't your CV.

'I don't think you realise how important this job is to me Thomas.'

He nodded understandingly. 'Well I'm sorry but you have a better life ahead of you. That job is pretty much over for you now anyway. Once we're married you'll have a large country house to attend to as well as this flat. What girl could resist?'

'Hang on Thomas, nothing is decided yet. What if I decline your kind proposal?'

'That would break my heart Elizabeth. Truly I would be devastated and it would be a no-win situation because in that case you'd have to leave anyway, just like Laura had to.'

She took a step back. 'Did you propose to her? She's married.'

'No, we never got that far, she missed her chance I'm afraid. But I was as honest with her as I have been with you and I couldn't allow her to continue working alongside me. Not everyone would understand and I hate the way ugly rumours can circulate. But her loss is your gain Elizabeth.'

'I'm not sure that we're compatible Thomas, not in the traditional sense, we don't really like the same things.'

'I like you and what you do for me. That's enough isn't it?'

'For instance, I like to laugh, and we don't do much of that.'

'We'll go to the comedy shows that you like if that's what you want. We'll go to the theatre all the time if you want.'

It was such a bizarre and unexpected turn of events that she needed time to think. She was crowded in with options and she was having trouble sorting them out. Up until now she had been going along with Thomas's sex games because they had little real impact on her and they'd been paying off in solid, bankable career development. The games never called for her physical involvement other than as a seductive jailer so her plan had been to keep it *going for a year or two and then take her glowing CV and achievements to some other company. Any kind of long term hook-up with Thomas had not* been on her map. It was an avenue that she'd never even considered, but on reflection it had some merit.

Thomas was looking at her expectantly and she needed to work out a strategy without him staring at her.

She pulled a strand of hair from her eye with a glittering silver talon and narrowed her eyes.

'Get in the cupboard,' she hissed, slapping the door with her palm. 'Now!'

'But Elizabeth, you haven't answered me.'

'I'll answer you when I'm good and ready Thomas, now put your hands behind you so I can tie them and get in the cupboard where you'll be as helpless as a lamb.'
Thomas did as he was told, the only difficulty was steering his erection into the cupboard without hitting it on the door.

Things had been looking up at Zingtastic since Steven had taken hold of his work life and started kicking some designer ass. In an effort to change his life he'd been into a book shop and bought a self-help book on being successful in the office environment, entitled '*Win in the workplace*'. It had been right next to another book called '*Lying your way to love and happiness*' but he had wisely chosen to ignore that one. In 'Win', lesson one was about freeing your potential by setting aside office paranoia and that was where he began his fight back. He tried very hard not to read negative things into the little signs he saw in the gestures and comments of his workmates and it had certainly helped to improve his mood. What was more was that the people around him seemed to be responding well to his new attitude. Katy had been in the coffee room twice while he had been in there, and both times had smiled. It was all good and taking the guidance of his book Steven believed that things were about to get a lot better. He had successfully buried all distractions and thoughts of comedy and scripts and really focused on the grown up job in hand. He kept the young designers on a short leash and made sure that they were at their desks and looking like they were working whenever Katy walked through. Even Adam had curtailed his YouTube addiction, at least in public.
And then, out of the blue Katy's right-hand woman, Julie, the Creative Director handed in her notice so that she could take a position with a bigger company. As she was going to work for a competitor she had cleared her desk and left the building by the end of the day. It was a shock and sad for Zingtastic, Julie had been great, but it smacked of opportunity to Steven. It was perfectly logical in his eyes that

he, the head of the design studio, could now be promoted to the vacant role. It all appeared to be falling into place, especially as Katy had been smiling so much in the coffee room lately. He had knocked the design studio into shape, he had shown his senior management potential, she liked him again and she needed a Creative Director.

In line with the instructions in chapter two of '*Win in the workplace*' Steven began to visualise his successful future in big, bright colours. He saw the following winning scenario: Katy would welcome him into her office with the biggest toothy smile, she would promote him to Creative Director, she would laugh and sign off his pay rise and he would travel home to Laura with a large bouquet of flowers and a bottle of champagne. It said in the book that if you visualised an outcome enough you would subconsciously make the adjustments that would make it happen. It was worth a shot, so Steven kept on visualising in a semi-trance at his desk. It did occur to him that he had been daydreaming about success all his life with very little positive effect and he couldn't really see how this was any different, but he pushed away the sour note. He closed his eyes and concentrated very hard on a mental picture of Katy shaking his hand. He saw her in glorious larger than life Technicolor pushing the contract across the desk towards him. He opened his eyes to see Katy frowning at him.

'Are you tired? Is the baby keeping you up?' she asked.
'No, I was meditating on the success of the company,' he replied lamely, but she had already moved away.

Laura picked up the ringing phone and heard the tell-tale echoing silence of an international call as it connected. Figuring that she was being hassled by a foreign call centre she was about to put the phone down when a distant American woman's voice said,
'Hi, is that Laura?'
'Hello? Yes it is.' She hated the delays inherent in

transatlantic calls. Why hadn't the technology wizards sorted that out by now?

'Hi Laura. This is Verona. I am very excited because I have a very funny script in my hand right now. It's called *Design Game*.'

Laura finally got up to speed. Verona was the American talent scout that Carries had mentioned.

'Oh yes. Good. You like it?'

'We love it. We're very excited about it. Does Steven have a UK agent?' Without missing a beat Laura replied, 'Yes he does, you're talking to her.'

FIFTEEN

Davis had missed the money when he'd first lost the Grand Hotel gigs, but his other business interests had nearly filled the gap now and the debt wasn't growing any more. He'd recently added a strong line in selling comedy memorabilia on EBay to his raft of money spinning ventures that included huge promotional inflatables imported from China. The enormous gaudy figures were literally springing up all over Scarborough and the other East Coast towns and for every one that did Davis got a cut.
But it wasn't mere business that made his pulse race, it was still comedy, even after all the knocks he'd taken. He'd finally admitted to himself that he was addicted to the buzz of it, and he knew that he was never going to be able to give it up no matter how badly it treated him. But in fact, comedy had started to be quite nice to him. The Railway Tavern club had grown from Wednesday nights to Friday and Sunday nights and it was exactly where Davis wanted to be. Every week he booked the acts and promoted the shows and every weekend he was the king-pin introducing the comedians and engaging the regulars in friendly banter. He had become a bit of a one man cult and he'd gained a reputation as an edgy performer who might just do anything at all. It was entertainment that you could never get on telly and the reality-TV jaded masses were beginning to flock in. Adult family groups had started to come back week after week and the atmosphere in the club was the best he'd ever known.
He also knew that some of the audience actually came along just to see him. He was rude, crude and irreverent and now that he didn't care anymore about management issues was ready to give it his all.
It was a small pool but he was the big fish and that was fine by him. The owners of the Railway were glad of the business and left him alone to run his club exactly the way he wanted to. It gave him a thrill that started on Thursday evening and

didn't go away until Monday morning when he got up to go to the job centre and sign on.

Davis knew he'd reached a new kind of Zen when Ray his old boss came in one night to see him. Davis didn't have him thrown out, but he didn't give him free entry either. Ray bought a drink and after some painful small-talk humbly asked Davis if he would work some freelance promotional magic on the hotels for the summer. They needed a splash and he knew Davis was the right man to provide it. Davis humbly told him to fuck off. Ray had simply smiled at that and told him how much he was willing to pay, thinking that it would change his mind. Of course there were certain conditions along with the money, plenty of constraints as there always were with Ray, and when Davis weighed them up against the freedom he would lose he knew the answer.

'I'm not interested mate. I'm happy here.'

'You're happy with this?' Ray was indicating the club around them, its peeling walls and shabby chairs which perfectly suited the scruffy clientele who were starting to cram in, many of them slapping Davis on the shoulder as they passed.

'Love it.'

'But it's a dump. Where's your ambition Davis? Where's that desire to be the top dog that made this country great?'

Davis pointed towards the small, slightly raised stage bathed by a single spotlight, its single microphone stand waiting as a challenge, like King Arthur's sword poised to be plucked from the stone. 'That's where the magic happens Ray, but there is no way that you could ever understand that.'

With a shrug Ray got ready to leave, but he was never quite able to let go of the idea that he was some kind of gangster.

'I hear you keep up the day job Davis, down at the DSS I mean. I wonder what they'd do if they find out about this club?'

'Probably the same as the VAT man would do if he found out where your imported booze comes from Ray or about the duty you don't pay. Or immigration about the illegals you use in the restaurant. They are vicious bastards those VAT men, they even want a percentage of your testicles.'

Ray winced and shuffled out, it was his honest belief that no man should ever, ever, under any circumstances, talk about tax out in the open.

Morgan was waiting in his dressing room, somewhere in the bowels of the theatre. Already it felt odd. He was used to standing near the back and being a secret part of the audience before a performance. He liked to judge the crowd and see who was in, it gave him a connection, but tonight, at Danny's gig he was going to walk out cold. He had opened shows on many occasions in the past but these days as headliner he was used to hitting a warm stage. A young man tapped on his door and led him up to the wings when it was almost time.

'I'll be taking you down to your seat in the audience after you've finished,' whispered the guy before leaving him alone. Morgan listened to the noises from the auditorium, the coughs and lowered voices and general gaggle of expectant excitement. He was trying to get a feel for the place but he just didn't seem to be able to manage it. He wasn't worried though, he knew that as soon as he stepped out into the lights he would feel right at home.

Eventually a well modulated broadcast quality voice boomed,

'Ladies and gentlemen, please welcome your host for the evening, Morgan.'

He walked steadily out to the mic in the blinding glare of the beam. They were ready to laugh or at least chuckle a bit and they were more than willing to let Morgan tickle them, but there was something strange about the space he found himself in. The audience were too far away. He was accustomed to seeing their every expression as they supped their beer and scratched their arses and he was used to using those interactions as fuel. Up on this stage he felt like he was in a goldfish bowl. He wasn't amongst them he was

isolated and it robbing him of some of his power. He felt oddly inhibited by the extra room and he couldn't get a sense of whether they liked him or not. They were laughing, but it was polite rather than raucous. He felt like he was giving a witty speech at a wedding rather than the vibe that he always aspired to which was that of telling jokes to his mates in the pub. Half way through his act, in a section that he knew so well that he didn't have to think about a dangerous thought seized his mind. What if this was the reason he'd never progressed? What if he wasn't up to the big rooms? It was the wrong time to be thinking and he pushed the thoughts away. He was hitting his time now, so he wound it down.
'You've been a wonderful audience, thank you so much. We're going to take a short break, time for you to get a drink and have a piss, in whatever order you want, and we'll be right back with the man you've all paid cold hard cash to see. Right after the break, Mister, Danny. Childs.'

When he came off stage the same young guy was waiting for him. If he hadn't been there Morgan might well have carried on and left.
'Well, done. Good work.'
'Really? Did it sound alright from where you were?'
'Oh yeah, it was great, now I'll show you back to your dressing room, you've got ten minutes to have a rest then when the house lights go down again I'll show you to your seat.' As they were walking back the kid said,
'God, I'm looking forward to seeing Danny Childs live. Aren't you? He's awesome isn't he?'
'Awesome.'
'He's brilliant, soooo funny.'
'Yes. Brilliant.'
'I think he's the best comedian in Britain right now.'
'Yes. The best.'
'He's...'
'Shut up kid.'

Morgan was taken to his seat next to the aisle, three rows from the front. He couldn't think of anything worse at that moment than having to watch Danny Childs tear up the stage. In his lap Morgan had the sheet with the heckles written out that he was supposed to shout out, he also had a tiny torch. It would have been easier if he'd learned the lines but he hadn't got round to it.

Danny was cheered out into the spotlight. He didn't seem to have any trouble at all connecting with the crowd or adjusting to the size of the venue. Of course everyone in the place apart from Morgan had paid to see Danny and Danny was what they were getting. The fans in the audience, the ones who'd seen him perform numerous times, of which there were plenty tonight, noticed that there was something a little off. Usually Danny fizzled with energy and his quips shot out in every direction like lightning bolts but this time he seemed a little subdued and low key. It was as if he'd just woken up and he hadn't quite got up to speed. Morgan sat impassively studying the act and waiting for his cue. The comedian eased into a quieter part of his show and then Morgan heard,
'What is it with people who won't shut up?' in the pause that followed Morgan dutifully shouted,
'I wish you'd shut up you foul mouthed loser.'
Danny was supposed to answer, 'Give it a rest mum,' as a lead in to a bit on how your mum never leaves you alone but instead he stopped dead in his tracks. He walked to the centre of the stage and said quietly,
'I wish I would too.' It wasn't funny and sounded hollow. Unease spread through the audience quicker than an airborne virus.
Morgan was mystified and thinking that Danny must have forgotten his line checked his sheet and shouted, 'Is swearing all you do? What's funny about that?'

The man sitting next to Morgan jabbed him with his elbow and hissed,
'Be quiet mate, I didn't pay to listen to you,' and then in the gloom he recognised Morgan as that night's first act. Incredulous he asked, 'What's the matter Morgan, jealous?' Morgan wasn't about to explain that he was playing his part in a ground breaking departure for the Danny Childs show. He wasn't going to try to convince the guy that this was actually intended to lift the show to new heights. He'd known this contrived heckling was a bad idea but he'd had no idea just how wrong it was going to be.
On the stage Danny was truly departing. He was standing slouched at the mic now. He looked as if he'd collapsed in on himself.
'I don't know,' he said shaking his head, 'any old shit will do for some people as long as there's swearing in it. They lap it up, the profanity. The rudeness, sexual references and naughty, naughty bad words. Words they won't let their children say.'
There were a few occasional nervous titters from audience members who were still waiting for the big punch line.
'But me?' he continued, 'What do they want from me? What do YOU want from me?' The painful expression on Danny's face left no one in any doubt that he wasn't joking now.
There was utter silence in the theatre. 'Actually it's true. People will laugh at anything as long as it plays to their own personal list of beliefs, hates and prejudices. As long as they can feel better by bringing someone else down. But they were ready to drop me like a piece of shit when it all got a bit too close to the bone. Then it wasn't so funny, was it?'
Someone shouted, 'We love you Danny.'
He snorted, 'Love me? You don't even know me. You don't know the *real* me. I don't even know who that is.'
The man next to Morgan was getting very agitated. 'What the fuck have you done?' he spluttered. 'You've killed him. You've killed his soul?'

'He's dying all by himself,' answered Morgan getting up to leave. 'When you die out there you're always alone.'
Morgan thought it best to get going before a bereft Danny Childs fan club formed a lynch mob. As he hustled away he heard Danny say,
'I don't want to do this anymore. It's just a stupid job and I don't want it anymore.'

As you walked away from the theatre Morgan wasn't quite sure what he'd just witnessed, it was a mental breakdown of some kind. He'd seen comedians walk off the stage many times, he'd seen anger and tears but he'd never seen anyone destroy the show business golden rule of soldiering on until they throw you off. He'd never seen anyone take a show that was going well and chuck it down the toilet. He started to wonder how it was going to play for him. Would he be hero or villain? All publicity was NOT good publicity and Morgan's natural tendency to see things in their worst possible light made him think that he might suffer a backlash. His best defence was to come up with some breathtaking jokes about the night he finished Danny's career and he'd already written a few by the time he got on his train.

Once the crowd had dispersed, too full of pity to riot, Danny came back out onto the stage and sat down next to the mic. Peter was sitting in a front row seat.
'So what was that?' he asked without rancour. 'You decided to piss it away without asking me? I've been working overtime to get you back up there and you decide to lie back down? If you wanted to retire why didn't you do it officially. You could have had a goodbye tour.'
Danny laughed. 'That would make you some dosh don't you think?'
'I'm thinking of you. You'd get closure. You'd get a chance to leave some doors open.'

'I don't want any open doors Peter. I've fallen out of love with stand-up. I've seen it and I've cracked it. I've resolved the puzzle and I think that's all I ever wanted. The thing is this isn't really me. The Danny they think they know is someone else.'

'Son, you're too clever for me, I don't know what you're talking about Danny, but I can tell you this, you're an idiot.' Peter got up and walked to the back of the theatre. As he opened the door to leave he shouted , 'You may be getting sued by some people by the way. You made commitments. Get yourself a lawyer.'

SIXTEEN

Before Steven had even put his bag down on his desk his phone buzzed with an internal call from Katy asking him to come into her office. This is it, he thought, the promotion. About time. They had been bumbling along without a Creative Director for a few weeks now, and Steven had been taking on more and more of the workload, so it was only right that something official was put in place at last.
He breezed into Katy's glass box and noticed that the blinds were closed.
'Shut the door please,' she said. He sat down in the chair opposite her. She smiled.
'Steven, as you know a few weeks ago Julie left us, which was a big change for the company and it forced us to really look at ourselves.'
When she said *us* she meant *me*, Katy always talked about decisions that she had made as choices of The Company, as in, 'The Company doesn't believe in Christmas bonuses.'
'Yes,' said Steven, 'I can see that.'
'So really Steven it was a huge opportunity for reappraisal. In short Steven, Zingtastic has decided to let you go. It's no reflection on your work, which has been pretty good, it's more a case of having a dynamic team of young designers who really don't need a manager.'
'Letting me go?'
'Yes. Sorry if that's a shock.'
'Not promoting me to Creative Director?'
She laughed at that.
'God, no. Is that what you thought? I don't know many Creative Directors who sleep at their desks.'
'I wasn't sleeping, I was visualising. It was part of a self improvement programme.'
'Did it work?'
'Not as such. Look Katy,'

She held up a strong hand. 'There's no point Steven. The company has made the decision it's out of my hands now.'
'But I haven't finished my work here. I feel there are some great things coming down the line, for me and the company. Each functioning for the mutual, er, benefit of us, and mankind?' He was babbling and it was embarrassing.
'Well look. We'll work out all the HR details later. Officially you are being made redundant. Your position is disappearing. You'll get your month's notice and of course I'll rely on you to act professionally in the hand-over. Adam will need to be brought up to speed on the outstandings. He's going to be in the new position of team leader now.'
Steven slowly stood up, he had an ironic smile pinned to his cheeks. Although still in shock, he had regained some of his poise.
'Katy, there's one thing that you really should have learned about me by now. You can never, ever rely on me to be professional.'
He walked back out to his desk, grabbed a few personal items and walked out without saying goodbye to a soul. He actually got quite a buzz out of an instant sense of freedom that he felt as he left the building, there was no panic or pain yet. It was like a cold day in the snow and he'd pissed in his pants to let the warmth comfort him.

Steven was in a trance, he couldn't understand what had happened and how badly he had judged the situation. He laughed at himself for being so stupid as to think he could possibly be getting a promotion. How pathetic, he thought, how deluded.
He couldn't go home and face Laura just yet, he needed time to think it through. She was not going to react well to hearing that he'd been fired what with a baby to feed and a mortgage to pay. She would naturally assume it was something to do with his slack attitude or his lack of focus. She'd think he'd daydreamed his way out of a job thinking about non-existent comedy gigs. As he walked through the

crowded London streets, not knowing where he was heading he suddenly felt very bad indeed. It was as if the piss had now become cold, so now he was freezing, and smelly too. What was he going to do? Go back to comedy? He couldn't go straight back to freelancing, he had let all his clients and contacts go, and by now they would have found new suppliers for their design needs. Sure, he could build up again, but it would take time and when you had a child the bills came in with crushing regularity.

Steven found himself in a park, he wasn't sure which one, but he saw an empty bench and sat down to watch the passersby. Busy people bustled along on their way to work, or on their way back from work. Everyone had a job, or so it seemed to him. Even the homeless people on their mobile phones probably had jobs. He delved into his pocket and turned off his own phone, he didn't want to speak to Laura. He sat for a very long time until the working morning was over, he wasn't hungry but at last it was time to go home. He'd let them down, his wife and child. They were relying on him to bring home a dead deer or at least some wildebeest that he's caught and he was going home empty handed. How could Heather respect a father who didn't have a job? A failed comedian without a job.

When he got home Steven squared his shoulders and took a deep breath before pushing open the door. He'd thought about going in crying to give himself the protection of sympathy, but it would have been worse in the long run, once Laura worked out that it was he was faking it.

He threw his keys onto the kitchen table and found Laura in the front room. He slumped next to her on the sofa. She looked like she was in a pretty good mood, smiling and happy and it hurt him that he'd have to trash that.

'Hi, where's Heather?'

'She's asleep upstairs, she went down early which is good because I really need to talk to you Steve.'

He nodded. Katy must have called her to fill her in, they were friends after all. She was still smiling though. 'I haven't told you about this but I've been doing a lot of work with your script, Steve. You remember that you said it was alright for me to run with it?' He didn't know where this was going so he simply listened. 'It's been tough, I had a steep learning curve but I kept at it and now we've had a lucky break. There's no such thing as luck but we've had one.'
'My script? The Design Game?' Steven wasn't really fully listening, he was simply delaying having to break his own news.
'That's right. As it stands it was a great effort but no one wants it as a TV show.'
'Right. That's what I told you...'
'But through some contacts I've made something else has come up. The ideas and characters and dialogue are great and it does seem to have a future as a film script.'
'You think?'
'Well if it was just me it wouldn't count but it's not me Steve, an American couple called Marti and Verona who's job it is to find and sell ideas to Hollywood. They trawl Europe for new, fresh creative treatments and then they know exactly who to go to with them. It's a long story and I didn't want to mention it because I didn't want to get your hopes up but in short they want to option it. That means that they pay to take control of the script and sell it as they want.'
He was befuddled.
'Not getting this. My script, the Design Game?' He had written off his sit-com long ago and thought that Laura had done the same.
'Yes. The Design Game. What's the matter with you, you seem out of it?'
'Just shocked. It sounds like a bit of a wind up and I'm not really in the mood for one.'
'Stop being so negative! This is good news. I've been negotiating and I'm keen that you don't lose all control so I have been trying to have you retained as a script consultant.

That way you keep an involvement. And more money. They'd get someone else to re-write it as a movie but you get a say.'

'They agreed with that?'

'Well, almost. You will have to go over for a meeting in L.A next week. They'll find you a hotel, but we'll have to stump up for the flight.'

'Ah, there had to be a catch.'

'It's not a catch Steve, it's an opportunity. Speculate to accumulate. It's an investment for God's sake.'

'They couldn't do it on the phone?'

'It's the first rule of sales Steve. Meet the people, meet the people and meet the people. That way you can charm them.'

'Right.'

'You go on your own for a couple of days and close the deal.'

'With Marti and Verona?'

'No. With a studio that they've provisionally sold your script to.'

She was grinning now. Finally she could reveal her secret. As the transatlantic calls and emails had speeded up and the deal had got closer she had found it harder and harder to keep her mouth shut, but superstition as much as anything kept her silent. She didn't want to jinx it. The producers had seen something quintessentially English about Steven's script and enough buried in it to make it saleable.

'Yeah?'

'Yeah.'

'It's a massive break Steve and I think we have to grab it. It could turn out to be the future that we've wanted. But if it works out and we're really going to give this a shot Steve, I think you might have to bite the bullet and give up your job. There's quite a bit of writing work to be done on the script and the character studies before we can get it in and you've only got two weeks to do it. You never really liked that job anyway, did you?'

'Er, not really.'

'It'll be a blow for Katy and I feel bad about that but that's business. Now, in the meantime I've been working on a back-up plan.'

'Back-up plan? Isn't this enough? It's the most amazing thing that's ever happened.'

'Well, let's not count our, you know, chickens. Anything could happen and if you give up your job you'll need some immediate income that you can generate, say in the evenings.'

'Like stand-up?'

The smile dropped from her face for a second, 'I know you love performing but it just didn't pay enough Steve.'

'True.'

'So, I've been talking to some corporate events people that I know. They are always looking for funny, entertaining after-dinner speakers. They are willing to give you a try out. They pay well, but you'd have to adapt your delivery. They like it personalised and, you know, about work issues. Photocopiers and stuff.'

'Wait a minute Laura. I appreciate all of this, I really do, but I don't get it. You've never liked my comedy, you never have.'

'That's not true. Besides it's all about perspective Steve. I'm seeing you as a product. I've always had a lot of confidence in your talent, at least in the fact that other people think you're funny, otherwise I wouldn't have spent so much time trying to push your work. For years I kept this household together financially, because I wanted you to have your shot. Well now I've been really enjoying the work I've been doing for you, and I've decided that I want to go into artist's management. I'm starting with you. I think I've got the talent for it, and it will mean that we can work together.'

'Well, the after-dinner speaking I understand, and I think it's a great idea, but this script thing, is that real?'

'Of course it's real,' she pulled a document from her briefcase which was sitting next to her leg. It was the same shiny case that had been rescued from the tube by Thomas Dalfin, the man who had made her see her husband anew. 'I

need you to sign a few things for me though, because I need to fax them over to the states.' She let him read. 'And then we need to write your resignation.'
He put the page down. 'There's something I need to tell you too Laura. We may be able to fast-track that bit.'

SEVENTEEN

It was a fabulous wedding, the kind of wedding you can only get when you have a very organised planner and you throw enormous amounts of money in every direction. Elizabeth was very good at planning and Thomas had the money, which would soon be her money too. The vicar had seen a fair number very pleasant nuptials but he was a particular fan of Jago Stellar the celebrity chef. He had several of his books and DVDs and was a big fan of his baked salmon with olives and anchovies recipe. Even men of the cloth can be star-struck and he found his gaze wandering from the text in front of him to the handsome, famous face in the congregation. The only disappointment was learning that Jago was not catering the reception which was being held on the lawns of Hanmore Castle. The bride was stunning, of course and the groom was smiling like someone who had truly found contentment and happiness. All as it should be for a union made in the presence of God, he thought. The service ran very smoothly except for one slight hitch that the vicar still couldn't make any sense of. At the point that the happy couple stepped into the vestibule to sign the register there was an inexplicable mix up of order and somehow the groom walked in alone, although the vicar was too far back to hear properly he could have sworn he heard the bride say, 'Now you're helpless' and with a little shove pushed the groom inside and quickly locked the door. In her huge white fluff ball of a dress, in the narrow corridor, she obscured the door for almost a minute before opening it to reveal a flushed but grinning newly married man. It must have been a pre-planned practical joke of some kind, and although he didn't approve of irreverence in church, he chose to ignore it in this case, especially as Jago Stellar came forward to shake his hand.
Thomas and Elizabeth had invited all their colleagues from Casket and Steel and Arthur Chase and his wife were

seated at the top table along with close family. It was both a wedding celebration and leaving do for Elizabeth but she was now looking forward to her life of leisure. The demands that Thomas made didn't repulse or trouble her and she'd found enjoyment in using her imagination to come up with new ways of confining and restraining him. Their relationship had developed and grown and so too had her power. Thomas had wanted her to sign a binding pre-nup agreement but she'd made him eat piece by piece through a hole in the side of a wooden crate. Amazing really, he'd done it and loved it. In fact he'd got so excited that she thought he was going to drill another hole in the wood.

Morgan was waiting to go on. He'd stormed this club in the past, but you could never tell. Different night and brand new crowd. He had some new material tonight worked out in the car and introducing new stuff always made him nervous. He could always dump it though and revert back to the tried and tested if it started to stall. He had to do a full fortyfive minutes tonight for which he would walk away with two hundred and fifty pounds in cash. He'd done four gigs already this week and he was due to do another tomorrow. It was a living. It was a job where he didn't have to take orders or get up early. He didn't have to sit at a desk and he didn't have to fill in reports or whatever it was that people in offices did. In his world he worked for an hour or less a day and he had enough to get by. He could do what he wanted to do most of the time as long as he kept on top of his diary. Travel was a bitch sometimes but it beat a daily commute. He didn't feel famous because he wasn't. For an hour a night he was almost a celebrity for anything up to a hundred people. He had respect from the other comedians because he'd been there and done it and he was doing something that plenty of others wished that they could do. He didn't get much excitement out of it anymore but the bottom line was that he couldn't do anything else. He didn't let it cross his mind that someday he might lose the touch, that he might get too old for student audiences, that he might start forgetting his jokes. He did worry that he might not get the precious TV break that would feather his nest, but he didn't think it was too late yet.

He couldn't see any problems with this lot tonight. As audiences went you could get surprises but these were a tame animal. Middle class, intelligent, reserved. They might not laugh too loudly but they wouldn't turn nasty. His new material on asylum seekers might go down pretty well, it was sympathetic and politically correct. He'd save the harder lines for another night.

He watched the compere come out onto the stage, and heard the warm applause for a comedian who was not in Morgan's class and he knew his waiting would soon be over, and then he'd be out there, and then it would be over and then he'd be in the car, and then he'd be somewhere else doing exactly the same thing again. It was a living.

EIGHTEEN

Danny had caused quite a furore when he'd given up comedy so publicly and not just with the crowd who had paid good money that night. Peter was right too, there were a whole bunch of people who had wanted to sue him for cancelled gigs and lost revenue. There were advertisers who were still running ads with his face endorsing them who were more than a little peeved that their image of comedy had imploded. There were fans who were, in their own words, absolutely 'gutted' and beyond consolation. People who had booked in advance and built their weekends around gigs that were now never going to happen. Reading through some of the messages, and the press, it appeared that Danny had ruined lives and plunged hundreds into misery. It was quite a responsibility, the unhappiness he had spread and Danny thought it best if he dealt with it head on. He knew that the way to deal with a problem was to face it, there was no long term gain in running away. But there was short term comfort, so he rang his sister to assure her that he was fine and then he bought a ticket to Greece on the first flight he could get. He checked his bank balance and calculated that if he lived very cheaply he could last for two, possibly three, years on what he had. His immediate plan was to fly to Athens and then go island hopping. He would make it up as he went along, take the boats and lose himself in the sandy Greek islands. He had no friends that he could take with him at such short notice but he didn't want company anyway. He wanted to be away from it all. He was going to act like a carefree student on a gap year.
He hadn't brought any guide books or information with him so he wasn't entirely sure which islands to visit, but he'd always had a certain romantic view of the Islands and at random he chose Mykonos as his first destination.

On the boat from the harbour to the island he was sitting watching the waves against the sides, wondering what he was doing when a voice asked,
'Excuse me? Are you Danny Childs?' He turned around slowly. He hadn't expected to be recognised by anyone, but especially not by aging travellers. 'I've seen you on TV quite often. You're very funny.'
'I was, I don't do that anymore.'
'My daughter is a big fan of yours. She's been to see you live quite a few times.'
'That's great.'
The guy looked about sixty, white thinning hair, not much of a tan yet and he hadn't quite got his holiday wardrobe sorted out. He was dressed as if he'd come from the office on a dress-down day.
'Look, I'm not going to bother you, I can see you want your privacy, I'm not a stalker or anything, but could I get a picture on my phone? I want to send it to Helen, my daughter, she'll be so jealous.'
Danny could tell that the best way to get the guy to leave him alone was to let him have the photo.
'Are you on your own Danny?'
'Yes.'
'Me too. I was in engineering for thirty-two years, same company. I was two years away from retirement and they made me redundant. I didn't want to go but they chucked me out. But I got a good pay-off so I thought, that's it, I'm off to Greece. They need the money over here,' he laughed.
'Cool.'
'I know what you're thinking, wife must be dead, but she's not, she just didn't want to come so I came on my own.'
'She didn't mind?'
'Couldn't wait to get rid of me. You get to this age and no one wants you anymore.'
They got one of the other passengers to take a picture of Danny and the man smiling together.
'So you Danny? Are you on holiday?'

He wondered if he was being teased. 'Sort of. Did you see the press?'

'Haven't seen any papers for weeks. I've been hopping round the islands.'

'Well, I wanted a break from comedy.' He looked at the old guy squinting at him in the sun. 'Couldn't take any more. Walked off stage in Putney. There's been a bit of a stink about it but I needed to do something else. Comedy is hard. Really hard.'

The white haired man shook his head. 'For fuck's sake. You should try working in a factory for thirty two years. Eight in the morning until six at night.'

'Yeah, I know but...'

'You twat. What I would have given for a life like you have.' Danny was taken aback, rocked in his self absorption. He was being aggressively heckled on a boat to Mykonos.

'But you said you didn't want to leave your job.'

'Yes, that's right. I didn't want to lose my job, I didn't want *them* to push me out but I hated every minute of it for more than thirty years.'

'Well, why did you do it then?'

'Because it's what we do us working people. We do things that we don't like to pay for the things that we do like.'

He was disgusted with Danny and turned away. Over his shoulder he said, 'You have a talent mate, a proper talent that people will pay for and you're ready to chuck it in. You think it's hard? You have no idea. You'll regret it.'

Danny went back to watching the water. Maybe the old fella was right, perhaps early retirement from the limelight was a bad idea. There had to be a reason why those old pop bands got together again after artistic differences had pulled them apart. Perhaps it all came down to the harsh reality of having to do real job if they wanted to eat.

For the first time since throwing his wobbly on the stage of that lovely theatre Danny thought seriously about what he would do when he ran out of money. He'd come from the office life so he knew what that was like. It might not be as bad as working in a factory but he couldn't go back to it. The thought returning and asking for his old job back almost made him jump off the boat and surrender to the inviting Mediterranean. The smug looks of those wonderful colleagues that he'd left so far behind as they asked him when he was going to hit his deadlines would be too much to take. He couldn't do that again, it made him want to cry just to think of it.

A lot of people when they were analysing the failings of others liked to talk about the self-destruct button and it seemed Danny had his finger jammed in his. But he wasn't living a wild, debauched life-style, drinking himself into trouble and offending everyone in sight, it wasn't that kind of self-destruct, the fun kind. Danny wasn't enjoying the Mickey Rourke school of self-destruct, Danny's was a snivelling, self-pitying whining form of damage. He was aware of his weaknesses and that only made them worse.

Danny was being tapped on the shoulder and he turned to see a different tourist, but again an oldster.

'Hi. Ian tells me that you are a famous comedian?'

'Well, not very famous.'

'I've never heard of you and I don't recognise your face, but could I have an autograph?'

'I guess, but why do you want a one if you don't know who I am?'

'It might fetch something on eBay.'

It was strange how quickly you could adjust to the unusual and start to treat it as a normal part of your life. Steven was sitting in a tastefully decorated room that had not one but three squashy cream coloured leather sofas in it. At one end of the room was a desk where a secretary was sitting typing and taking calls. She had an American accent, which was not out of place because Steven was IN LOS ANGELES, CALIFORNIA, U.S.A. He was very quietly flicking through a magazine, but in his head he was shouting it. I AM IN L FUCKING A. HOLLYWOOD. It was incredible. He'd been

waiting for fortyfive minutes stuck to this sofa but he didn't mind. He was here to see some studio people about his script, which they had already optioned, that is they had paid some money for, and in Steven's book that meant that they liked it.
It had been a very exciting but exhausting couple of weeks. His head was spinning but he was trying to act as if he was calm and in control. Another man came in through the same door that Steven had used he crossed to the secretary, checked in and then came to sit on the sofa opposite Steven. At a guess he was in his fifties with long white hair to his shoulders and a straggly beard. He looked a bit like one of those cowboys who has never been on a horse. He smiled pleasantly at Steven.
'Hi, are you here to find out if your dreams will come true?' Steven wondered if he was a religious nut, but he thought carefully about the question.
'I suppose I am. I've come about a script that I've written.'
'So you're another writer. Me too.'
'I can't really call myself a writer, I've only done this script, I'm more of a comedian really. In fact I'm more of a graphic designer than a comedian or a writer.'
'Right, sounds like you're from Britain. Ok, well if you're here about a script then I'm afraid that makes you a writer whether you like it or not. I know we're a bunch of assholes, but you are in the club buddy.' He was still smiling to show that this was a joke.
'Thanks. Are you here about a script as well?'
'Yeah, in fact I've got a couple of things in development with these guys.'
'Wow.'
'Yeah, sounds impressive doesn't it but let me tell you, I've had a lot of stuff in development over the years and not much makes it onto the screen.' He could see by Steven's face that it wasn't what he wanted to hear. 'But the good news is that you still get paid. I make a nice dollar out of films that never get made. They don't want to lose out to

another studio so they pay. Take my advice, when you get in there,' he pointed at the door at the other end of the room, 'be prepared to compromise and you'll be great. If you try to hold on to your artistic integrity and you want to cling to your vision, then it may not work out so good.'
They fell into a little silence until Steven spoke. 'It feels like before a comedy gig. Always the nerves crippled me when I was waiting to go on.'
'Well you'd better get used to it because the waiting never stops in this business my friend and when it does it means that you're dead. The best thing you can do is find a way to enjoy the waiting. If you can crack that then you're made.'
Eventually the receptionist said, 'They're ready for you Michael,' and the guy got up. He winked at Steven.
'Best of British luck,' he said in a poor English accent.
'Remember, compromise pays the bills.'

When Steven was finally called into the office he was met by two well groomed young men who didn't look old enough to be wielding any power. They weren't the large bullet-headed moguls that he's been expecting. Mark and Howard, invited him to sit down at the long empty meeting table.
'Good to meet you at last Steve,' said Howard. 'I hope your hotel is comfortable?'
'It's perfect thanks.'
'We've been really excited about this project I can tell you.'
'Ever since Marti and Verona brought it to us we've talked of nothing else.'
'Really? That's brilliant.'
'It needs some changes of course but it's exactly what we're looking for.'
'That's right. Have you heard of Harry Steadford? He's one of you guys, right? He's famous over there?'
'Yes. Harry Steadford, quite a well known comedian, in fact I have a friend who started in the business with Harry.' Steven was prepared to mention Morgan as a friend in this context in an effort to ingratiate himself with Howard and Mark.

'Ok, well Harry has been making an impression with US audiences with a TV show about Britain called *Britain's Underbelly* on cable. You know the show?'

'Yes, I've seen it. Many times. Watch it all the time.' Steve noted that the babbling was kicking in.

'He's been a hit.'

'Well, long story short, there's been a lot of interest in the guy, there's a feeling over here that he could be huge and we need a vehicle for him so we can see if he can carry a movie.'

'Your script, The Design Game, has some of the elements that we need.'

'We like the idea.'

'We like the title.'

'And the crazy man in a design studio.'

'At the moment it's too short but once we move the location to New York and make all the characters Americans apart from Harry,'

'And we make it more accessible, which the writers will do, we might be able to do something with it.'

Howard, checked the sheet of paper in front of him.

'Now, part of the option deal that your agent negotiated was that you would be retained as script consultant.'

So, apparently Steven now had an agent and it was his wife.

'That's right. And I've got to say that I'm very excited about that.' Being excited about things seemed to be a requirement and Steven was more than happy to admit that he was.

'Which, we are very comfortable with,'

'We love that,'

'but what we need Steve, is for you to sign a release.'

'We will of course look at any ideas that you come up with, but we'll retain the right to only use the ones that we deem to be appropriate.'

'And you can't sue us later,' they both laughed at this, as if it wasn't their main concern.

Steven held up a finger. 'Can I just ask, what is the likelihood that the funny ideas that I contribute, as script consultant, will be used?'
'Honestly?'
'Very little chance. We will have a professional comedy scriptwriter working on this and we will treat it with full respect, but once it's in the cooker, you probably won't get to mess with it.'
'Why did you bring me all the way here?'
'You've got to meet the people Steve and for this project to fly what we need to know for sure is that it's clean and that further down the line once we've invested time and money we're not going to get any interference.'
'That's right, so we are free to work with it without fear of litigation. You'll retain a credit as a script consultant but we don't really need any consultancy.'
'So this is really about you giving me some money, me having the title of script consultant and you doing whatever you damn well please with the script?'
'Yes,' said Mark.
'Yes,' said Howard.
'Where do I sign?' said Steven.

Laura was very impressed with herself and what she'd been able to achieve. She had faced the odds, taken on the unknown world of entertainment, grappled with Hollywood, and won. At least as long as Steve played his part at the meeting over in L.A. she would win. Steven had a talent for screwing things up but surely he'd make the most of the truly once in a life-time opportunity that she had given him. But even if the film chance fell through her back-up plan was shaping up nicely. Steven had done one event so far, given an after-dinner speech and hosted an internal awards ceremony for an insurance company. Having sat through a few and knowing how these things usually ran she'd made sure that he'd been fully prepared, that he'd worked in some lines that featured some of the employees names and kept it all very corporate. All the sexual stuff had to be dropped from his old stand-up act, as did the very sweary bits, (you could never under any circumstances use the C word at a corporate), but a lot of the rest of it they were able to adapt. Now the cheque was in and she'd looked at the finances and if she could continue to get him out there Steve should easily make what he had been making at Zingtasatic. It would also mean that he could be around to take up the child care during the day. They could get rid of the nanny and save that money too. If he could spend some time writing scripts or doing whatever script consultants do as well he might really hit his earning potential. But that was all in the future and right now she had a number of events managers to mail with Steve's CV and the glowing reference from the plastics gig. Damn, she'd caught herself, she was trying not to think of them as gigs but as after dinner presentations and speeches.

Danny stretched his legs out on the sand and smiled at the way his angst had melted away after only a couple of days of stress free living. No one else had recognised him and now he was starting to get a little bit bored. He turned on his mobile phone and waited while it worked out where he was in the world. He pressed the speed dial and waited for the inevitable voicemail to pick up.
'Hi, Peter. I know that you don't want to talk to me but I wanted to tell you that I'm thinking of coming back and honouring some of those commitments that haven't already cancelled. I needed to get my head straight, so I had it twisted straight by an engineer. I also found out the real Danny Childs is. Now, I'd like to cut down on the number of venues waiting to string me up. If you want to be part of that then let me know, it might get you out of some jams too, I don't know. I'll be heading back in a couple of days, so if I don't hear from you by then I'll assume you don't want to know. Cheers. Bye.'

It occurred to Danny that back in dreary London his message might well sound like the ravings of a mad man, but for the first time in months he felt good about himself. He nudged Julio, the gorgeous boy who had helped Danny voyage of discovery into himself, literally. Julio was lying on his back catching some sun, that frankly his tan didn't need. Come to Greece and find a Spaniard.
'It was Peter's answer phone,' he told Julio, throwing the mobile onto his blanket.
'Will he help you?'
'I don't know, but it doesn't matter really.'
'If I come back to London I can help you maybe?'
Danny grinned, 'That would be cool.'

Steven had finished his very important meeting by signing everything that they wanted him to sign in exchange for money plus Howard and Mark's vague and unconvincing promise to use his further script ideas as and when he sent them in. In a perfect world Steven would have had every contract scrutinised by a top entertainment lawyer first but he'd never done that with any contract he'd ever signed in his life so he wasn't about to start now. Not when his main fear was that they would change their minds and take the money away.
It was his last night in America, the complimentary hotel room was about to run out and his flight was the following morning.
'So, what are you going to do with your last night in town Steve?' asked Howard ushering him towards the door to make room for the next crucial meeting.
'Not sure.'
Mark piped up, 'Gotta say that you have some real funny lines in that script Steve.'
'Thanks.
'I hear you used to do stand-up, is that right?'
'Yes, for a while I did that.'
'Like, professional?'

'I got paid gigs, yes.' He saw no reason to be totally honest at this point, it was all small talk anyway. If they went away with the idea that he was almost as big as Harry Steadford surely it could only help his cause?

'You know if you wanted to catch some live comedy we've got a bunch of great clubs here. There are quite a few on Hollywood Boulevard, not just the famous ones either, like the Comedy Store and the Laugh factory.'

Mark started to get excited, 'In fact, I have a friend who owns a little club over there. I could give him a call. You know I'm sure you could get an open mic spot?'

'Well, I'm not so sure about that.' Suddenly Steve's pulse was racing and the sick nervous feeling surged through his gut. It was completely unexpected but it was the full waiting to go on effect.

'It would be a blast wouldn't it? Let me give him a call. I'll tell him I've got a hot-shot British comedian over for him.' He was already dialling before Steven could object.

NINETEEN

Steve had to wait until one thirty a.m. for his spot to come up, by which time there were no more than ten people left in the club. It was a club in the sense that it was a bar, with a mic at one end and the obligatory back-drop sheet announcing 'Live Comedy'. The club owner didn't remember getting a call from Mark, but it didn't matter,
'Sure, you can go on,' he said shrugging, 'What do I care? I've got an open spot at real late o'clock.'
He took a pen from his pocket and poised over the running list.
'Name?'
'Chicken, Steven Chicken.'
Steven saw the game, while you were waiting around you were bound to buy some drinks. The last proper gig that Steven had done was nearly three years before. You couldn't count the plastics after-dinner speech that Laura had arranged for him, that was more of a scripted presentation. He'd got paid more for that then any performance he'd ever given, but a corporate was a different animal. It was a trained dog, it had teeth and it might use them, you wouldn't leave it alone with a small child, but it was fairly safe. A stand-up gig was a wolf. It looked like a pet but it was essentially a wild animal and it would savage you if you treated it with any less than full respect.
Steve watched a succession of very poor comedians come and go, each one believing that as they lived in the city of entertainment they were no more than a step away from stardom. As the night wore on the crowd thinned and the tired businessmen lurched away from the tables. Steven was drinking, but not heavily. It was mad really here he was, the world at his feet in this vibrant, energetic city and he was wasting his time in a comedy club. But he had an itch and in this anonymous outpost was the best place to scratch it. Eventually, after a very skinny young kid had finished his

depressing bit on being a single guy, the owner who was also introducing the acts looked at his list.

'Ok, next up we have a real treat for you. The last act tonight, we have a guy who has come all the way from London, England to be with us tonight. So, here he is, Steven Chicken.'

There was no applause, what was left of an audience were severely jaded by now.

Steve walked out into the single spot light without any nerves at all. He savoured being in front of the mic for a few seconds before he spoke.

'Hello Los Angeles. Wow, I've waited a long, long time to say that. Years in fact. So here's the thing. Sometimes you wait so long to go on that when you do finally get on – you've forgotten what your point is. But tonight my point is to say goodbye.'

He swept his hand wide to indicate every one of the completely disinterested early morning drinkers.

'To you, my loyal fans who have travelled so far to see me die on every stage in the UK, the pain is finally over. From the ancient pubs of East London to the dives of Wallsend in Newcastle. Here in L.A. the home of comedy, movies and drive-by shootings I've finally realised I'm sick of dying. I'll put this in a way that you movie buffs will understand. It ends tonight. Here and now. Right here, right now. This time it's personal. On stage no one can hear you scream. One man against the world. And finally, of course, *I won't be back.*

Chicken walked from the stage and made his way out through the tables without a single regret, without a backward glance, without being noticed and without payment. He had a plane to catch, an agent to thank and a daughter to push round in a buggy. Living the dream.

TWENTY

When the film was finally released two years later it was called 'Mishmash' and it featured not one single line of Steven's dialogue and it bore no recognisable similarity to Steven's script. It did however carry something financially important, the on-screen credit of, 'from an original concept by Steven 'Chicken' Spring. Steven and Laura sat as invited guests at the London Premier, watched an energetic Harry Steadford leap around like a loon and then waited until the final credits had almost disappeared before glimpsing the name. In many ways it was a job well done.

The money they received in a thrilling one-off payment paid for a spanking new kitchen and there was something else that Steven insisted on. For toddling Heather he bought a large weathered climbing frame for the garden made from an aged and rustically attractive cargo net. It was a symbolic purchase for Steven and it formed one of the Hollywood stories that Steven now told to his high-paying corporate after-dinner audiences three nights a week. Buying the weather beaten net with the film money pretty much summed up show business to him. Money for old rope.

END

Printed in Germany
by Amazon Distribution
GmbH, Leipzig